The Confrontation

A TRILOGY BY DAVID CAUTE

1
THE DEMONSTRATION
a play

2
THE ILLUSION
an essay

3
THE OCCUPATION
a novel

Dedicated with love
to the memory of my father
and to the future of my sons
Edward and Daniel

BY THE SAME AUTHOR

NOVELS

At Fever Pitch (1959)
Comrade Jacob (1961)
The Decline of the West (1966)

PLAY

Songs for an Autumn Rifle (first performed 1961)

POLITICAL STUDIES

Communism and the French Intellectuals (1964)
The Left in Europe since 1789 (1966)
Editor: Essential Writings of Karl Marx (1967)
Fanon (1970)

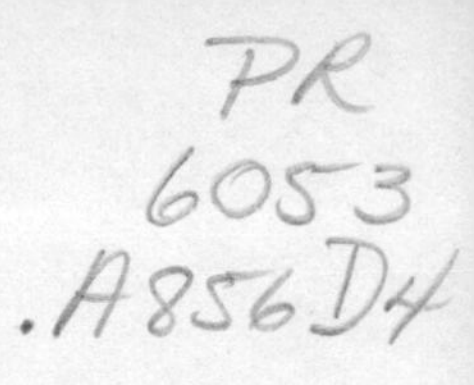

THE DEMONSTRATION

A PLAY

David Caute

ANDRÉ DEUTSCH

First published 1970 by
André Deutsch Limited
105 Great Russell Street, London WC1

Printed in Great Britain by
Ebenezer Baylis and Son Limited
The Trinity Press, Worcester and London
ISBN 0 233 96278 6

Preface

The Demonstration is the first work in a trilogy consisting also of an essay, *The Illusion*, and of a novel, *The Occupation*. Each part of the trilogy is autonomous and can be read (or, in the case of the *The Demonstration*, performed) without reference to the other parts.

In what sense, then, can three separate works, each written in a different genre, be said to comprise a unified trilogy? If I were to attempt here too explicit an answer then I would betray a central proposition which is this: that nothing said *about* a play or novel, however accurate, carries the same meaning as the play or novel itself. In other words, meaning is conveyed *through* a particular dramatic or fictional structure and has to be discovered immanently, from within the work. This notion is expanded at a theoretical level in *The Illusion*; and I hope to have applied some of the arguments contained in that essay by the way I have written the play and the novel. (Which is not to suggest that theory has all along been master and practice, slave. On the contrary, the interaction of the two has been intense.)

But the following remarks may prove helpful:

In both *The Demonstration* and *The Occupation*, Steven Bright is the central character. He is also – or so I have pretended – the author of the essay, *The Illusion*. In both the play and the novel Bright is depicted as an intellectual of the Old Left who finds himself suddenly confronted by the tidal wave of student revolution associated with the New Left. On both occasions Bright's conflict with his own students results in the confiscation then destruction of his manuscripts and notebooks. One of these manuscripts is in fact *The Illusion*, an essay concerning politics, the theatre and the novel. That it will nevertheless prove possible to publish a text already destroyed is a riddle easily solved: the cautious Bright had made a wise practice of quickly distributing carbon copies of everything he writes to his friends and publishers. Whether one applauds or deplores this simple technological manoeuvre will perhaps depend on one's political sympathies.

In *The Demonstration*, Bright is forty-five years old (although a particular actor will 'make' Bright as much as Bright 'makes' the actor.) He is a Professor of Drama teaching in an English university. In *The Occupation* he emerges as rather younger, a novelist and modern historian who is spending a year in an American university as a Visiting Professor. Viewed in the light of these facts alone, there are two different Brights. But knowing him well (our paths have often converged), I can testify that he is no less convinced than I that what joins the Bright of the play to the Bright of the novel is more, far more, than a name shared in common.

In naming Steven Bright as my central character, and not the student revolution and its fictional representatives, I have made a painful choice dictated, I would like to believe, by honesty. As for the political implications of this choice, I know them only too well. They afford me no contentment. But I surely do not have the right to allow myself the good conscience which I have so persistently denied to Bright.

David Caute

Production Note

The entire play should be performed within a single set. This set represents the stage of the University theatre.

Whatever description a particular scene may be given in the text (i.e. 'The Office of the Dean' or 'Trafalgar Square'), it should always remain abundantly clear that the necessary or suggestive props have been superimposed on the basic set – the stage of the University theatre.

I have no wish to dictate the design of this basic set. It should, however, contain a screen, centre and downstage, onto which slides can be projected. Patrick Robertson's set at the Nottingham Playhouse made excellent use of shutters, or slats, on both sides of the stage, which could be opened and closed when a character pulled a lever. If this aspect of design is not adopted, then some equivalent adjustable device must be devised to represent the barrier between the theatre within and the world outside.

Cast List

The first production of this play was presented by the Nottingham Playhouse Company at the Nottingham Playhouse on November 19, 1969, with the following cast:

Max	*Robert East*
Ann	*Cherith Mellor*
Frank	*Nicholas Clay*
Tom	*Alec Heggie*
May	*Penelope Wilton*
Bright	*Marius Goring*
The Dean – Dott – Marty	*Francis Thomas*
Assistant Dean – Dooley	*Bruce Purchase*
The Women's Dean – Demonstrator	*Anna Wing*
Professor Cross	*Jon Whatson*
Aston – Pedro – Lightfoot	*Trevor T. Smith*
Vietnamese Woman – Hippie Student	*Lois Baxter*
Officer – Reporter – Guerrilla – Pack	*Bruce Myles*
Tirade – Marines Captain	*John Manford*
Clive – Student	*Martin Thurley*
Sally – Student	*Helen Lloyd*
Garfield	*Donald Gee*
President	*Frank Middlemass*
Shane	*Peter Whitbread*
Marko	*Peter Eyre*
Second Worker – Hippie	*Leo Dolan*
Girl Student – Woman – Hippie	*Jane Fox*
Youth – Student – Negro Militant	*Michael Jeffries*
Student – Man – Hippie	*Jay Truscott*

Reporter – Student – Negro Militant	*David Plowright*
Student – Vietnamese Man – Militant	*Christopher Wood*
Radio Voice	*Tony White*
Student Guitarist	*David Clough*

Students: *Rupert Auchterlonie, Michael Barnard, Irwin Bottomley, Chris Brierley, Susan Carter, Wendy Cole, Robert B. Davidson, Sara Davidson, Lynne Davey, Beverley Eades, Bob Evans, Simon Garbutt, Stu Harrison, Nicolette Hughes, Judy Kelham, Andrew Mackay, Pauline Martine, Cassandra Mellor, Jim Miller, Lawrence Morgan, Chris Penter, Carol Robins, John Ruddy, Alec Sabin, Kevin Cole*

directed by	*Stuart Burge*
associate director	*Charles Savage*
settings by	*Patrick Robertson*
costumes by	*John Elvery*

Act One

SCENE ONE

The stage of the University theatre. Enter MAX BROWN, *a student actor, wearing a raincoat. He closes the shutters, blots out the daylight, turns up the stage lights. Pacing about, he works himself into the role of Coriolanus.*

MAX: Like a dull actor now, I have forgot my part,
And I am out, even to a full disgrace. Best of my flesh,
Forgive my tyranny . . .

He is interrupted by the entry of ANN MARTIN, *a student actress who is* MAX's *girl friend. She too wears a raincoat.*

ANN: Greetings, Coriolanus, it's raining.

MAX *immediately reverts to the role of Coriolanus.*

MAX: Mother! [*Addressing* ANN *as if she were Volumnia*]
Best of my flesh,
Forgive my tyranny, but do not say,
For that forgive our Romans. O a kiss
Long as my exile, sweet as my revenge!

He leans forward to kiss ANN (*Volumnia*) *who thwarts him.*

ANN: Methinks the spirit of this filial kiss too incestuous. [*She laughs*]

MAX: [*Kneeling, gravely*] Of thy deep duty, more impression show
Than that of common sons.

ANN: [*Moving away*] Coriolanus was a fascist gangster. You are too nice for the part, my love.

MAX: [*Still kneeling, feigning sadness*] Like a dull actor now, I have forgot my part . . . [*He jumps up*] Come to the movies tonight.

ANN: Too much work. What about final exams?

MAX: I'll buy you a plate of delicious crispy chips at the Golden Egg afterwards.

ANN: You'll buy them and I'll pay. I know my Max.

Enter FRANK, TOM *and* MAY, *student actors, all wearing raincoats.*

FRANK: Hey Max, have you seen the wall of the new workshops? Someone wrote 'Engineers are Sods' on it.

MAX: Was 'engineers' spelt right?

FRANK: Mostly.

MAX: Then we know the engineers themselves are in the clear. [*Running his hand over* MAY'S *stomach*]. Either you're smuggling pot in there, darling, or you're pregnant.

ANN: Leave her alone.

FRANK: We ought to discuss *Pentagon 67*, you know. This play is beginning to worry me.

MAY: But why, Frank? I think it's tremendously exciting. It's going to be the best thing we've put on.

FRANK: You think everything Steven directs is the best thing we've put on.

TOM: *Pentagon 67* is becoming an elaborate diversion.

MAY: From what?

FRANK: From reality, from our own situation here.

MAX: Talking of which, Ann, this epitome of all virtues, feminine, philanthropic and academic – is in serious trouble.

TOM: The Women's Dean rides again?

ANN: She said I was corrupted by pride.

MAX: And by other things. Wait till I give evidence.

ANN: She's threatening to suspend me for a year.

TOM: The bitch. They're all bastards and bitches.

FRANK: All the more reason to do our play instead of *Pentagon 67*.

ANN: Steven will never agree to it. He is devoted to *Pentagon 67*.

FRANK: It's his ideal of committed drama. Undramatic and uncommitted.

ANN: That certainly goes for Steven's own intervention at the end. What does he call himself?

MAX: Steinblitz, Professor Karl Steinblitz. [*Imitating the part of* STEINBLITZ] 'I hear the words "Che Guevara" pass frequently from your mouths. I hear some of you calling yourselves urban guerrillas. But Guevara was a technician of revolution: do you deserve that title?'

STEVEN BRIGHT, *forty-five years of age and professor of drama, has entered to overhear this. He is wearing a raincoat and carries a briefcase.*

BRIGHT: Do you? . . . Steinblitz is meant to be sixty-six, not a hundred and sixty-six. I suppose it all seems the same from your vantage point. [*pause*] Or should I say disadvantage point?

MAY: [*Embracing him*] Are you going to be alright, Steven?

BRIGHT: [*Embarrassed, releasing himself.*] Alright, child? Why shouldn't I be alright? [*He opens and closes the shutters, testing them*].

MAY: Because of the President. I mean the rumour is going about that the President of the University is furious about our end-of-term production.

BRIGHT: The President approves only of plays whose authors have been dead for three hundred years. In his opinion, the value of contemporary art can be judged only by – posterity. In fact it was not the President who made me late. It was the Women's Dean.

ANN: Oh God. What did she say about me?

BRIGHT: It took her some time to get around to you. Her first salvos, as usual, were directed against my failure to award you all proper grades. For the Women's Dean, the human race is first divided vertically, into male and female. This unholy split accounts for all the sin and grief in the world. But apparently some compensation is to be found by dividing mankind horizontally, into Grades A, B, C, and, best of all F.

ANN: But what did she say about me, Steven?

BRIGHT: [*Vaguely, not interested*] Oh . . . nothing of any consequence. Troublemaker . . . corrupted by pride . . . usual sort of thing. [*More animated*] I have something to show you. [*Calls into wings*] Slide! [*A projection of the Pentagon appears on the screen at the back.*] I think that's an excellent view. [*He moves about the stage.*] The soldiers will stand here . . . the rope will be just in front of them here . . . and you lot, the savage militants, here. What do you think?

Silence.

FRANK: Very pretty. The slide, I mean.

Silence.

BRIGHT: [*Sensing their unease, but passing it over*] Right, Max, Ann, let's run through the final scene. Inside the Pentagon. Ready?

MAX *and* ANN *prepare to play the scene with some reluctance.* BRIGHT *claps his hand. The stage darkens and a projection of a corridor inside the Pentagon appears on the screen. A* YOUNG MAN *and a* YOUNG WOMAN *both run on stage, as if in the corridor, and then move forward hesitantly.*

YOUNG MAN: We've made it. We're inside.

YOUNG WOMAN: There were no guards. Where were the guards?

YOUNG MAN: Gone home, I guess. Or maybe . . .

YOUNG WOMAN: On the outside it has five corners, but inside it has no shape at all, just corridors and more corridors.

YOUNG MAN: Each room is like the next, nothing but telephones and piles of paper.

YOUNG WOMAN: But no people. No people anywhere. The place is empty.

YOUNG MAN: There's nothing to lay your hands on, nothing to seize, no one to grab hold of. Nothing to do.

YOUNG WOMAN: Then how does it work . . . how does it run the war if . . . ?

Instant blackout. Pause. All lights go up.

BRIGHT: Good. That is to say . . . better. It should be almost as if you are floating under water.

MAX: [*Becoming himself again*] One question.

BRIGHT: What, Max?

MAX: Why does your play have to end on the word 'if'?

BRIGHT: Why not?

FRANK: Ending the play on that note suggests the whole demonstration was a waste of time.

TOM: You make her say, 'how does it work?' In other words, how does the Pentagon work, does it work at all, does it really exist?

BRIGHT: Ann?

ANN: The trouble is, Steven, the play poses many more questions than it answers. You end up feeling you're going nowhere.

BRIGHT: [*Upset*] Do you? Do you *really*? You all speak as if with one voice. [*He claps his hands and the Pentagon projection disappears; then takes a text from his briefcase*] And this . . . so tactfully dropped on my desk in the name of you all . . . is *your* ideal of committed drama?

MAX: Have you read it, Steven?

BRIGHT: Yes.

ANN: Did you like it?

BRIGHT: It has remarkable qualities.

MAX: He didn't like it.

FRANK: That was predictable.

BRIGHT: The title intrigued me: *The Demonstration.* I suppose you inherited that idea from *Pentagon 67.*

TOM: We got the title from daily life . . .

FRANK: As we live it.

ANN: Perhaps you can suggest ways of improving it. The characterisation, for example.

BRIGHT: Since the play is about yourselves, the characterisation can hardly be faulted.

MAX: [*Turning away*] Irony.

ANN: What about the plot, the sequence? Do you think it sustains its tension?

BRIGHT: It does, oh it does. I was gripped throughout. Early skirmishes between students and university authorities; extremely vivid. Confrontation – absorbing. The outcome – irresistible.

TOM: But?

BRIGHT: Is there any coffee, May?

TOM: [*Insistently*] But?...

BRIGHT: You are familiar with my point of view. [*Opening and closing the shutters*] There, out there, is life. And here in this box we create art. But life remains one thing and art another. Art should not imitate life, it should translate life. And that is quite a different thing. [*Pause*] This play of yours is dramatic.

MAX: Ought it to be dull and boring?

BRIGHT: If my trousers were to fall down suddenly, that I suppose would be dramatic. But that is not what I mean. The kind of drama you have cooked up is the kind which tries to make itself a carbon copy of real life. Precisely the banal naturalism I have always warned you against. [*Gently*] Why must you involve your audience totally in the action? Why do you want them to forget they are watching a play? Why must they believe it's all real? This is the twentieth century not the nineteenth.

FRANK: The society we live in is real. The authoritarian regime which runs this university is real. We are real.

BRIGHT: If you people are so wedded to reality, then why waste your time on theatres, costumes, scenery and plays? Why bother about art? A play is a play, a fiction, a fiction. But in this play of yours naturalism, as usual, quickly leads to romantic extravagance. Your experiences become indistinguishable from your wildest dreams.

TOM: Lenin identified with his dreams. So did Fidel.

BRIGHT: They didn't muck about in theatres.

MAX: Okay, what shall we do – *Waiting for Godot*?

BRIGHT: How seriously are you opposed to going ahead with *Pentagon 67*, as planned?

FRANK: Seriously.

TOM: Seriously.

MAX: Seriously.

BRIGHT: I'm not prepared to abandon weeks of effort just like that. Nor do I think this play of yours will work. But I take it you won't be convinced unless we try.

TOM: That's right. We won't.

BRIGHT: I suppose we could always extract from your play a series of basic situations, then explore them in artistic terms. A kind of theatrical safari.

MAX: Which presumably, means discarding the play itself and the logic of its development.

TOM: [*To* BRIGHT] Are you worried about the President's reaction? He wouldn't like our play, would he? It would decidedly alarm him, wouldn't it?

BRIGHT *turns away*, *furious*.

ANN: No, Tom, that was uncalled for.

MAX: Shall we vote on it?

BRIGHT: Vote? Since when were universities run by votes? In any case, five of you can hardly speak for the whole Drama School.

MAX: We represent the general will. Those in favour of doing our play *and* sticking to the text . . .

MAX, FRANK, TOM *and* ANN *raise their hands.*

MAY: [*Close to tears*] I don't like voting. It's sadistic.

BRIGHT: [*Petting her*] Don't worry, child, just abstain. One lives longer that way.

SCENE TWO

The office of the Dean of Students. The DEAN, *the* ASSISTANT DEAN, MAX, FRANK *and* TOM.

DEAN: You are late.

ASSISTANT DEAN: Ten minutes late.

MAX: Public transport has become so unreliable under a socialist government. Hand it back to private enterprise, I say. [*He reaches for his cigarettes*]

ASSISTANT DEAN: No one gave you permission to smoke.

DEAN: A complaint has been lodged against all three of you by the City Police. They are aware, as I am aware, that you have all been in trouble before.

MAX: We hereby apply for legal aid, a writ of *habeas corpus* and permission to smoke.

DEAN: On Tuesday last, outside the gates of the Conway Motor Corporation, you were arrested for holding an unauthorised demonstration. Unauthorised by the Police; unauthorised by me.

MAX: On the following night, between the hours of two and three, I turned over in bed without first obtaining a licence to do so. I ask that this offence be taken into consideration.

ASSISTANT DEAN: Try and grow up, Mr Brown.

DEAN: I have nothing against demonstrations.

ASSISTANT DEAN: Provided they are authorised.

DEAN: We view most applications favourably.

ASSISTANT DEAN: When applications are made.

DEAN: When students get involved with the police, it is we who come to the rescue. This is a benefit and a protection which others do not enjoy. But the benefit involves certain obligations.

TOM: We were holding a discussion with the car workers about racism and the war.

FRANK: Your war.

MAX: How can we apply to you for permission to demonstrate against your war?

DEAN: I did not bring you here to engage in a discussion on current affairs. Rules are rules. Kindly conform to them.

FRANK: The rules are bad.

DEAN: [*Rising*] Very possibly. No one compelled you to come to this University, and no one is compelling you to stay.

SCENE THREE

The office of the Women's Dean. THE WOMEN'S DEAN, ANN.

WOMEN'S DEAN: Now you know the rules, Ann.

ANN: Yes, Miss Latham.

WOMEN'S DEAN: In any single fortnight, provided it be term and not vacation, and excluding religious festivals, bank holidays and epidemics, a woman student shall eat twenty out of twenty-eight meals in college, not counting breakfast, which she must attend if not consume, to show that she has passed the night. Correct?

ANN: Yes.

WOMEN'S DEAN: And you have missed five lunches and six dinners in a single fortnight.

ANN: The truth is, I find college food uneatable.

WOMEN'S DEAN: We have a complaints book.

ANN: I know: It's an institution – like the bad food and the high price.

WOMEN'S DEAN: We have staff problems. We are dependent on foreign labour. Native labour is not attracted by the wages we offer.

ANN: Perhaps a cafeteria system would be best. With a cafeteria you can choose your own food according to your own taste, budget and timetable.

WOMEN'S DEAN: Such permissiveness would weaken social life here.

ANN: The men have a cafeteria. Perhaps we could eat with the men.

WOMEN'S DEAN: All wedges have thin ends.

ANN: The other thing is, we can't help noticing that the food which goes up to the High Table is very much superior to our own.

WOMEN'S DEAN: The faculty pay more. They know more. They earn their living. [*Rising*] You will in the course of the coming month attend not less than fifty out of fifty-six main meals in college, not more than thirty to be lunches and not more than thirty to be dinners. Understood?

ANN: Is there no appeal?

WOMEN'S DEAN: Only to me.

SCENE FOUR

A lecture room. PROFESSOR CROSS, MAX, ANN, FRANK, TOM, MAY *and four other* STUDENTS. PROFESSOR CROSS *is old and short-sighted.*

CROSS: Who is not here? [*Peering*] Who is here? [*Peering*] Very well. Where did I get to last time?

ANN: To the laws of history.

CROSS: [To ANN] You, young lady: how many laws of history are there?

MAX: You promised to tell us. That's why we're here.

CROSS: There are three. Three. First law: history has no laws. Take that down.

FRANK: The nature of the first law seems to preclude the existence of any others.

CROSS: What? You are no philosopher, young man. For if history has no laws, the first law itself must be false, which opens the way for laws two and three. Second law: take this down: periods of change are followed by periods of stability, which in turn are followed by periods of stability.

MAX: Of change, you mean.

CROSS: I know what I mean. A period of stability is one in which the civilized and culturally mature elements in society prevail. A period of stability, on the other hand –

ANN: Of change, you mean.

CROSS: You just take it down. [*He peers at her*] I like you. You have a fine head of hair, young lady. Don't let your young man get away with it. A period of change is one in which hitherto and deservedly inferior strata attempt in their folly to usurp roles and responsibilities for which they are innately unfitted.

MAY: Please, Professor, does that mean that progress is bad?

CROSS: If it were progress, it wouldn't be bad. A historian must avoid tautology. Bad is a moral word. Moral questions have no place in the study of history.

TOM: What is your view of the French Revolution?

CROSS: Typical of the French.

FRANK: Of the Russian Revolution?

CROSS: Typical of the Russians.

MAX: Of the English Revolution?

CROSS: We had the good sense and political genius to get our period of change over and done with at an early date. Whereas the French keep having theirs again and again.

TOM: Are wars inevitable?

CROSS: Wars solve population problems, they stimulate trade and industry, and they inspire great works of art. Take that down.

ANN: But after a nuclear war there will be nothing to be solved, stimulated or inspired.

CROSS: The study of the past is not a horoscope.

FRANK: When does the past stop and the present begin?

CROSS: In 1914.

TOM: Is that date equally relevant for the peoples of Africa and Asia?

CROSS: I am not an anthropologist. Nor am I an archaeologist, a geologist or a sociologist. I am a historian. Next week I shall address you on the role of great men in history. [*He gathers his papers and leaves the room, muttering*] One can say so little in an hour . . .

ASTON *enters now. He is brisk and energetic, with the style of a business executive. A complicated chart is projected on the screen behind him.*

ASTON: Hello again, are you tuned in and turned on? Right, let's go. Programme one: distinguish between critical-constructive and critical-destructive attitudes towards prevailing norms and identity roles. The graph behind me illustrates on the basis of income differentials the curve of inadequate normative integration and functional identification amongst socially crystallized leadership groups.

MAX: [*Standing up*] Excuse me, couldn't we have a short critical-constructive break for coffee? I feel inadequately integrated and normatively differentiated.

ASTON: The future won't wait, Mr Brown. Indeed,

tomorrow is already here. Right. In view of the failure of traditional knowledge-repository and value-creating groups to respond positively to new media and mind-manipulating innovations, our technetronic future in the fast-arriving post-industrial age dictates the maximisation of elite incentives leading to a standardisation of control patterns based on a computerised calculation of behavioural structures necessary for a dominant role in a world consumer market in which monopoly is the only calculable alternative to annihilation. This requires and demands the rapid reorientation of fiction, poetry, theatre, art and music away from outmoded circuits of private sensibility towards eulogistic celebration of space travel, supersonic booms and North Sea Gas. It also demands abandonment of anachronistic and obsolescent techniques of knowledge retention and distribution. (That is to say, if the entire store of information in the world's libraries be taken as one quadrillion bits, and if the information stored within the printed media be assumed to double every twenty years, the already anticipated solution is the creation of integrated computer teams, each unit storing one thousand million bits of information, the whole system yielding a direct access memory that can respond correctly to any question even before the question is posed. In other words, in the future the questions will be dictated by the answers.) All this necessitates that as the managers, leaders, planners, controllers and mind manipulators of the post-industrial age, you must de-condition obsolete moral and ideological structures from your nerve systems, replacing them by authoritarian reflexes which obliterate tendencies towards uncompetitive contemplation and compassion for weaker elements. Is that clear?

MAX: Excuse me. I feel sick.

ASTON: Go to bed and take two aspirin.

MAX: What I mean is – I don't want to be alive in the world you describe.

ASTON: Then go to bed and take a bottle of aspirin.

He strides out cheerfully.

MAX: He must be the first human being to have received a heart transplant from a dying robot.

[*Author's note: if Aston's speech is cut — as at Nottingham – the words within the brackets should be omitted*].

SCENE FIVE

The office of the Women's Dean. ANN *is seated. The* WOMEN'S DEAN *is pacing about.*

WOMEN'S DEAN: What is the primary purpose of a university education, Ann? Explain to me in your own words.

ANN: My own words are the only ones I have.

WOMEN'S DEAN: Quite.

ANN: Do you mean under the present social system, or ideally?

WOMEN'S DEAN: I would probably find Plato's vision of utopia more absorbing than your own.

ANN: And more acceptable, I expect. The philosopher king idea has always appealed to dons.

WOMEN'S DEAN: That is really no way to speak to me. At one time I regarded you as one of our most promising and single-minded students. Clearly you have over-extended both your capacities and your emotions. I see that you are now a member of no less than eight voluntary associations, some of them political in character, some of them philanthropic, and all of them time-consuming.

ANN: Life is time-consuming.

WOMEN'S DEAN: A university and 'life', as you call it, are

not the same thing. Here you enjoy the unique privilege of studying under scholars of exceptional distinction – a privilege coveted by many less fortunate than yourself.

ANN: Should that comfort me?

WOMEN'S DEAN: Can't all this philanthropic fervour be contained until after you have graduated?

ANN: [*Losing her poise*] I find it hard to contain myself when I discover that all the coloured women in my neighbourhood have to cut their own hair. 'Sorry, dear, but we don't do your sort of hair.' I find it hard to contain myself when I learn that a black family is paying ten pounds a week for one unheated, vermin-infested room. I find it hard to contain myself when I see pictures of napalmed children in Vietnam. Children without skin. I find it hard to contain myself when I see some old wretch begging for bones in a butcher's shop. No, I can't contain myself until after I have graduated.

WOMEN'S DEAN: But what of your career prospects, once so promising?

ANN: I want to be an actress.

WOMEN'S DEAN: So Professor Bright has told me. I suppose he allows you to neglect your other studies. [*Pause*] Professor Bright is very popular with his students.

ANN: Yes he is.

The WOMEN'S DEAN *clenches her fists and paces the room.*

WOMEN'S DEAN: I suppose that nowadays a would-be actress feels marvellously absolved from all moral values and restraints. No doubt Professor Bright encourages you to 'liberate the instincts' in the service of your art!

ANN: I'm sorry, I don't –

WOMEN'S DEAN: [*Stopping abruptly*] Are you pregnant?

ANN: [*Shaken*] Pregnant? No, why?

WOMEN'S DEAN: We must be thankful for small mercies. I can only tell you, Miss Martin, that I am shaken, deeply shaken, by what has been brought to my attention. [*Wrings *her hands*] How little modern girls understand what they are risking!

ANN: [*Confused*] But – I take the pill.

WOMEN'S DEAN: You mean you premeditated this act in cold blood?

ANN: Not very cold. [*Her own anger rises*] I simply don't see why it should be anyone's concern but mine.

WOMEN'S DEAN: I have a responsibility to your parents.

ANN: My parents are both dead.

WOMEN'S DEAN: All the greater my responsibility to them.

ANN: I'm twenty-one.

WOMEN'S DEAN: You are a student! A student! [*Pause*] I have to think of the other girls.

ANN: Most of them do it. The only crime is to be found out.

WOMEN'S DEAN: Slander does not improve your position, Miss Martin. I had hoped to find some evidence of contrition in you. I find none.

ANN: [*Beginning to cry*] I've been having periods for eight years. What do you expect me to do?

WOMEN'S DEAN: Show some self-respect. The College has a right to expect –

ANN: [*Crying*] The College is like the Pope: it should mind its own bloody business.

WOMEN'S DEAN: [*Drawing herself up*] Very well. I shall recommend to the President that you be expelled from the University.

SCENE SIX

The office of the Dean. DEAN, ASSISTANT DEAN, MAX. MAX *is swathed in bandages.*

DEAN: Well, well.

ASSISTANT DEAN: Mr Brown is observed on Monday last, at

the hour of one in the morning, attempting to scale the wall of Barton Road Women's Dormitory.

DEAN: Is then observed to have impaled himself on the spikes which have been put there to impale him.

ASSISTANT DEAN: Is then seen to fall, accompanied by part of the wall.

DEAN: But you, Mr Brown, will no doubt prove to us that all this rising and falling was conducted in the service of world peace.

MAX: I am a keen outward bound enthusiast. I hoped to win the Duke of Edinburgh's Award.

ASSISTANT DEAN: And the fact that two hundred young women were asleep behind the wall did nothing to promote your enthusiasm?

MAX: Only one hundred and ninety-nine were asleep.

DEAN: Where and when – if ever – do you work?

MAX: I work in the magnificent new library whose seventy-six seats so generously encompass the needs of our five thousand students.

DEAN: [*Holding up a magazine*] Have you ever seen this before? It's an unauthorized student magazine called *Opinion*.

MAX: I concede that the title is subversive.

DEAN: In the latest issue appears an article under your name, entitled 'Amusements Guide'. I quote: 'Professor Cross on Continuity and Change. The lecturer is normally inaudible and often closer to sleep than anyone except his pupils. Occasional sound waves can be de-coded to indicate his preference for continuity over change.'

ASSISTANT DEAN: What right have you to publish such remarks about a distinguished scholar who has loyally served the History Department for twenty-five years?

MAX: I'm not disputing his pension rights.

DEAN: Professor Cross's books enjoy an international reputation.

MAX: I know. Unfortunately, teaching just isn't his thing.

After all, we are constantly reminded that we prosper in a competitive society based on free consumer choice. Why shouldn't students form their own Consumers' Association and publish their own *Which?* ?

DEAN: Because, Mr Brown, a student cannot properly evaluate what he does not know. In view of your past misconduct, I shall recommend to the President that you be suspended for one year.

SCENE SEVEN

The office of the Women's Dean. WOMEN'S DEAN, ANN, MAY *and four* GIRLS.

WOMEN'S DEAN: [*Staring horrified at a sheet of paper*] Sixty-five!

1ST GIRL: Only sixty-five were prepared to sign. Each of these girls has done what Ann did.

2ND GIRL: If the offence is the same, the punishment must be the same.

WOMEN'S DEAN: It's not possible. Sixty-five! You must take me for a complete fool.

1ST GIRL: Each of us is prepared to give you chapter and verse.

2ND GIRL: And if not to you, to the press.

WOMEN'S DEAN: The press! Have you no loyalty to your College?

1ST GIRL: Only if it inspires loyalty.

WOMEN'S DEAN: Many young girls don't understand what they are saying. A minor indiscretion after a dance or party, and they imagine —

MAY: Oh no, Miss Latham, most of us are quite systematic about it. As they say in the army, we like to have it regular and we have it regular.

WOMEN'S DEAN: Good God. Regular. [*Pause*] Regular. [*Pause*] Good God.

IST GIRL: Expel Ann, and you must expel us all.

WOMEN'S DEAN: Must I indeed? Why, the College would be virtually depopulated. Let me remind you that questions of discipline are the concern of the Faculty and only the Faculty. The Charter of the University makes it abundantly clear where ultimate authority lies. The tail cannot wag the head.

ANN: Very well, then, it's war.

IST GIRL: If you expel Ann, we'll hold a press conference –

2ND GIRL: Boycott all lectures and classes –

3RD GIRL: Occupy the buildings –

4TH GIRL: Turn our beds into barricades –

They are interrupted by the entry from the wings of BRIGHT. *He opens and closes the shutters.*

BRIGHT: Well! The *pétroleuses* of the Paris Commune could have learned a few tips from you lot. [*He imitates the* GIRLS] 'Boycott lectures and classes'; 'Occupy the buildings'; 'Turn our beds into barricades.' [*Wiping his brow*] Whew! Is this scene really authentic? Or necessary?

ANN: Certainly it is. Do you feel threatened?

BRIGHT: I have no love for the Women's Dean. But I don't believe she could behave so stupidly.

ALL THE GIRLS: But she has!

WOMEN'S DEAN: It's true, Steven. She has recommended to the President that Ann be expelled.

BRIGHT: [*To* ANN] Then why are you wasting your time in rehearsals? Why aren't you packing your bags?

ANN: We intend to resist.

Pause. BRIGHT *scratches himself.*

BRIGHT: [*Shouting*] Everyone on stage!

The other STUDENT ACTORS *of the company enter and seat themselves on stage round* BRIGHT.

BRIGHT: Ann: you insist that all this has actually occurred?

ANN: Of course.

BRIGHT: Because you were found in bed with Max?

ANN: Because Max was seen leaving my room at six in the morning.

BRIGHT: [*To* MAX] And you: are you also to be expelled?

ANN: Not at all. One rule for the girls and another for the men.

FRANK: In fact, Max, Tom and I are threatened with a year's suspension.

MAX: For multiple injuries to the academic body politic.

BRIGHT '*steps back*'. *He is intellectually and emotionally cornered. The attitude which he will adopt does not depend on any quick decision; on the contrary, it is built into the man. He is, of course, appalled by the stupidity of the university authorities. But he can no more afford to identify with his students than he can with the authorities. No words – only a certain kind of silence – can convey that the crisis is planted here.*

BRIGHT: Well! The sacrifices that you people make for your art! This child [*He indicates* MAY] identifies with her fictional role to the point where she puts a real child under her dress instead of a pillow. When art mimics life, the result is banal. When life attempts to anticipate art, the result is ludicrous.

Silence.

MAX: Steven, are you overtired?

ANN: That is the most perverse distortion of the truth that I have ever heard.

MAX: [*Speaking slowly*] I don't follow.

BRIGHT: Of course you follow. You go to elaborate lengths to get yourselves embroiled in all sorts of improbable situations —

ALL: Improbable!

BRIGHT: You tie lethal ropes round your necks simply to provide documentary material and spiritual preparation for a melodramatic extravaganza. [*Cries of protest*] I fully accept your basic case against the Women's Dean. But that doesn't mean that I have to abandon my sanity and accept your glowing portrait of yourself as Joan of Arc facing her inquisitors. And what is the result? A perfectly peaceful, not to say somnambulent, English university has been transformed on this stage into the Sorbonne, Nanterre, Berkeley and Columbia all rolled into one! Not on this stage: I forbid it.

TOM: It is forbidden to forbid.

BRIGHT: I forbid you to forbid me to forbid in my theatre.

FRANK: *Our* theatre.

VOICES: *Our* theatre!

BRIGHT: [*Less incensed than he pretends*] What, what! I'm not going to be treated like that raucous mob treated Jean-Louis Barrault when they invaded the Odéon. I'm quite capable, even at this late stage, of recommending to the President that your talents are better suited to the study of Early Middle English and domestic science than to the stage.

Tempers rise.

FRANK: Make your bed with the President and the Dean. We don't need you.

BRIGHT: [*Exploding*] Don't you? Perhaps you're a bit short on history. When I first arrived here there was no School of Drama and no theatre. I was appointed, quote, 'to teach dramatic texts and to explicate the language in its oral aspects', unquote. It took me three years to get acting recognised as a part-time option on the curriculum – *your* curriculum. And you tell me that you don't need me. [*Pause*] Why did you call your play *The Demonstration*?

FRANK: Because that's what it is.

BRIGHT: I'm not out of sympathy with your general aims.

But you've gone the wrong way about it. There are two types of demonstration; there is demonstration look-look and there is demonstration bang-bang.

ANN: But Steven, you give us no credit. If we weren't interested in demonstration look-look, as you call it, we wouldn't be interested in performing our play.

BRIGHT: Whatever impels the militant in you, whatever leads you to clutch the burning cross of fire, let the actor in you subtly thwart and contradict.

FRANK: What it all boils down to is that the professor and the radical in you are in a state of civil war.

Murmurs of agreement. But BRIGHT *is apparently not touched by this thrust.*

BRIGHT: Tomorrow afternoon we'll do a quite simple theatrical exercise. Theme – demonstration.

MAX: There is a march to Trafalgar Square tomorrow afternoon.

BRIGHT: Another demonstration bang-bang. Against what?

MAX: The war.

TOM: The Vietnam War.

BRIGHT: The war. You have three weeks in which to rehearse and perform your end-of-term production. The war has at least two years to run.

FRANK: You sound a bit like the Dean.

BRIGHT: I am a bit like the Dean. Very well. We'll do it tomorrow morning.

The STUDENTS *leave the stage.* MAY *stays behind.*

BRIGHT: [*To* MAY] Are you really pregnant?

MAY: [*Close to tears*] You're cruel, Steven, very cruel.

Silence.

BRIGHT: I suppose it could be psychosomatic.

SCENE EIGHT

The stage of the university theatre. BRIGHT *stands waiting, to the side of the stage. Enter a bearded* GUERRILLA, *carrying knapsack and rifle. He wanders about, obviously lost, then consults a map. He does not notice the arrival of* PEDRO, *a peasant.*]

GUERRILLA: This mountain area is said to be thinly populated. Thin is the word.

PEDRO: [*Calling across*] Have you seen my goats?

GUERRILLA: [*Startled, reaching for his rifle*] What? Who are you?

PEDRO: Pedro, a simple peasant.

GUERRILLA: Fraternal greetings, comrade. I am Nameless, a highly-trained guerrilla. Where have you been?

PEDRO: Been?

GUERRILLA: I have spent four valuable weeks searching for the impoverished masses of this province and you are the first human being I have set eyes on.

PEDRO: [*Shrugging*] If you want my opinion, nobody lives around here.

GUERRILLA: Precisely. Our strategy is to avoid populated areas. And now – you must carry my message to the toiling rural proletariat.

PEDRO: Too dangerous.

GUERRILLA: Carry it in your head, if you have one. You are . . . You are . . . [*He searches for the words. The first impression is that the actor has forgotten his lines. This impression is reinforced by the* PROMPTER'S *voice.*]

PROMPTER'S VOICE: You are brutally oppressed by an evil system.

The GUERRILLA *now clearly refuses his lines.*

GUERRILLA: I don't want to go ahead with this.
BRIGHT: [*Stepping forward*] Why the hold-up?
PEDRO: It's insulting, degrading.
GUERRILLA: We're not in sympathy with this exercise.
BRIGHT: That's why I devised it. It's an alienated demonstration of a demonstration against alienation.
GUERRILLA: It's counter-revolutionary, objectively speaking. A bourgeois audience could take comfort from it.
BRIGHT: A bourgeois audience never recognises the source of its own discomfort. When it's morally disturbed, it complains of obscenity; when it's politically challenged it proclaims the play trivial. In any case, there is no audience. [*He gestures towards the auditorium*] We are alone with our own deviations.
GUERRILLA: The lines stick in my throat.
BRIGHT: Imagine an athlete training for the Olympic Games. Does he spend all his days galloping downhill? No: he forces himself through the deepest sand dunes he can find. He thrives on resistance. He knows that self-indulgence will not transform his dreams into realities. Please continue.

He withdraws to the side.

GUERRILLA: [*Reluctantly*] Our strategy is to avoid populated areas. And now – you must carry my message to the toiling rural proletariat.
PEDRO: Too dangerous.
GUERRILLA: Carry it in your head, if you have one. You are brutally oppressed by an evil system. The Government is the tool of the landowners. The landowners bleed you white, taking from you everything you produce. The State and the Army exist to crush your struggle for emancipation.
PEDRO: Very true.

GUERRILLA: [*Disconcerted*] You know all that?

PEDRO: We also know that we are backward illiterates, not yet radicalised, and still in the grip of obscurantist and quasi-feudal mystifications. That is to say, we have an inadequate grasp of the dialectics of revolution in the Third World.

GUERRILLA: Che Guevara! In that case . . . But how –

PEDRO: Another bearded one came this way three years ago.

GUERILLA: Was he tall – like so?

PEDRO: Taller than the corn when it dances with the harvest moon. That is how we talk round here. Our prosaic adaptions and modifications of primitive religious songs are of considerable anthropological interest.

GUERRILLA: Yes, well. But I tell you, Pedro, much has been learned these last few years. Do you appreciate that the whole armed force of the landowner's state, when confronted by the anger of the united, militant and revolutionary masses, is nothing but–

PEDRO: – a paper tiger? Of course.

GUERRILLA: Already the common soldiers of the Army are deserting to our side.

PEDRO: True. I am myself a part-time militiaman.

GUERRILLA: [*Reaching for his rifle*] What!

PEDRO: Calm yourself. It's my day off. Now I must find my goats before dusk.

GUERRILLA: [*Seizing him*]. History first, goats later. Pedro, I will show you, I will demonstrate. Any time now an Army patrol is due to pass this way.

PEDRO: [*Running away*] Good luck.

GUERRILLA: [*Catching him*] Courage, comrade. Now observe. We hide behind this – this small mound of earth.

PEDRO: I cannot see it.

GUERRILLA: Down, down. [*They lie flat*] Our greatest weapon is surprise. And our morale is rising to its revolutionary peak. How do you feel?

PEDRO: Sick.

GUERRILLA: I will demonstrate. Ssh. Here they come.

Enter an army patrol of five, shambling and dishevelled. They are led by a fat OFFICER *wearing a comic opera, ice cream outfit, heavy with braid and medals. He smokes a huge cigar.*

1ST SOLDIER: We are lost, Comandante.
OFFICER: Lost, scum? What do you say, dog?
GUERRILLA: [*Whispering*] After many years of experience we learn to distinguish the officers from the men.
OFFICER: Forward, pigs and curs! I smell guerrilla scum, filthy materialist bandits. Forward!

The patrol advances a few paces.

GUERRILLA: [*Raising his rifle*] Never fire too soon.
PEDRO: Nor too late.
GUERRILLA: Now! [*He pulls the trigger, but nothing happens*] Che Guevara, my cartridges must be damp.

He wrestles with the bolt. PEDRO *covers his head and begins to pray. The patrol passes by. The officer steps on* PEDRO *and the* GUERRILLA, *without noticing them.*

OFFICER: [*Departing*] The ground is very soft in these parts.
GUERRILLA: Jerusalem –
PEDRO: Wasn't built in two thousand years. To tell the truth, after such episodes I always undergo severe attacks of obscurantist, quasi-feudal mystification. Farewell, brother. [*He moves away, then stops. He rebels. He speaks now as a student actor*] It can't end like this.
GUERRILLA: I agree. [*He hesitates, then takes resolve*] Wait Pedro, I have found a dry cartridge. All is not lost.

BRIGHT *intervenes briskly.*

BRIGHT: You've found what?
GUERRILLA: [*Sulkily*] A dry cartridge.
BRIGHT: But the patrol has passed.
GUERRILLA: They always come back. They move in circles.

[*To* PEDRO] Quick, down.

BRIGHT: 'Behind this small mound of earth.' Idiots.

GUERRILLA: [*To* BRIGHT] Stand aside or you may get shot.

BRIGHT *does not budge from centre-stage. Enter again the army patrol.*

OFFICER: Ha! I smell the blood of filthy materialist Marxist guerrilla. [*He reaches for his pistol. The* GUERRILLA *shoots him down.* BRIGHT *recoils from the blast*] Aaaagh! I am hit. Dogs, curs, swine, hold me up! [*The* SOLDIERS *stand back*] Traitors! I die! [*He dies writhing*]

GUERRILLA: [*Rising*] Brothers, comrades, sons of toil, you are free!

SOLDIERS: [*Embracing*] We are free, free!

A horde of PEASANTS *rush on, carrying red flags.*

PEASANTS: We are free, free, free!

GUERRILLA: Che is dead, long live Che! Viva Che!

ALL: Viva Che! Viva Che! Viva Che!

BRIGHT *intervenes by opening and closing the shutters. The chanting subsides.*

BRIGHT: [*Smiling*] Who's for Early Middle English and who's for a crash course in Domestic Science?

MAX: [*A soldier*] Guerrilla campaigns may fail nine times out of ten. It's the tenth occasion we're interested in.

BRIGHT: Quite. But is art interested? What is art?

GUERRILLA: It can be optimistic.

BRIGHT: Can it be thirsty or tired? Can it make love?

PEDRO: We don't understand you.

BRIGHT: Please don't say 'we'. You aren't Russians. [*Pauses*] You are merely actors.

GUERRILLA: Actors are no longer obedient puppets; nor are students. For you, a double threat, no doubt.

BRIGHT: I'm a petty-bourgeois academic terrified of a

changing world. If it smooths your path towards Armageddon to believe that, smooth away.

ANN: [*A peasant woman*] Steven, why don't you come with us to Trafalgar Square this afternoon? Get the smell of grease-paint out of your lungs.

MAY: [*A peasant woman*] Do come with us.

MAX: [*Sardonically*] Perhaps a mild clout from a fuzz truncheon would help dispel false consciousness.

BRIGHT: I warned you that your own play wouldn't work. But you insisted on learning the hard way. If we progress at this speed there will be no end of term production at all. [*Silence*] I suppose we could always revive another play – a play which promises to reconcile the claims of commitment with the demands of art: *Pentagon 67*.

STUDENTS: No!

BRIGHT: A pity, particularly in view of the guaranteed presence of the talent scouts from the professional theatres on such occasions. [*Silence*] As a teacher I can only advise you to follow your consciences while remaining safely on the ground floor of your art. [*He pulls a lever and a picture of Trafalgar Square appears on the screen.*] It's perfectly possible, you know, to march to Trafalgar Square without ever stepping outside this theatre.

SCENE NINE

The Demonstration. On the screen, a projection of Trafalgar Square. The words 'A Walk in the Sun' are superimposed on it during the parade which opens the Demonstration: young mothers with prams, militants carrying banners, Christians rattling collection boxes, hippies, etcetera. As they pass round the stage and gather, the inscription

'Citizens Discuss' is superimposed on the screen. Four bystanders, two men and two women, have watched the parade. The guitarist plays more softly.

1ST WOMAN: What do they really want, anyway?

1ST MAN: I'm an old soldier: Dunkirk, Anzio, Normandy. If you ask me, what these youngsters need is the blitz.

2ND WOMAN: It's the taxpayer who pays.

2ND MAN: It's not like the thirties anymore. In those days it was the head of the house who marched. We used to march in our Sunday best. We knew what we wanted.

1ST MAN: [*Moving off*] If this is what democracy means, I say we can do without it. Mind you, I'm all for democracy.

1ST WOMAN: Some people seem to have nothing better to do.

They exit under a bingo sign which flashes on and off. The stage lighting changes abruptly. The militants gather for the Japanese hop, chanting 'Ho – Ho – Ho Chi Minh!' 'LBJ – Out!' 'Fascism – Out!' 'War – Out!' Out of this crowd emerge ANN *and* MAX. *They move into an empty space but* ANN *continues to offer leaflets as if she were surrounded by people. The inscription on the screen is now: Young Love.*

ANN: [*Attempting to distribute leaflets*] Women's Solidarity Campaign against Racism and War! Create a better world for your children! [*She thrusts a pile of leaflets into* MAX'S *hands*] Be useful.

MAX: [*Halfheartedly trying to distribute them*] Women's Solidarity Campaign against ... [*To* ANN] What's it against this time? [*He sighs*] It's no use. I just don't look like a woman or a campaign.

ANN: [*Working through the 'crowd'*] Make the world safe and sane for your children!

MAX: Miss Martin, I wish to make a prophecy.

ANN: I'm not listening.

MAX: The way things are going, Max's highly desirable mistress is soon going to be a professional absentee from Max's highly desirable bed. And why? Because she will be not only national secretary of the Solid Women, but also local co-ordinator of Oxfam, chairlady of the Common Sense Citizens, regional regulator of Start It and travelling activist of Stop It. She will pitch her sleeping bag on the doorstep of 10, Downing Street and stage a starve-in which will make Mahatma Gandhi look like a swollen glutton.

ANN: And highly desirable Max?

MAX: Highly untouchable Max will write a bestseller called *The Politics of Frustration, or Self-Abuse: the Road to International Peace*! [*He attempts to distribute leaflets*] Common Sense for Women! [*He fails*] Stop It! [*He grabs and kisses her*] Is Nelson's Column a phallic symbol?

BOTH: No, it's the other way round!

MAX: Precisely. What really rouses you at the sight of a six-foot phallus are your childhood memories of Nelson's Column.

ANN: Six-foot, Max?

MAX: Ah, you've never seen me really try. Listen: Why are we standing in the road?

ANN: Because the audience prefers the pavement.

MAX: Correct. I love you.

They run back into the real crowd. The militants throw out a challenging cry. The lighting changes abruptly. MAX *leaps forward and freezes in a dramatic posture. Enter now* SALLY, *a beautiful cover-girl, and* CLIVE, *a dandy photographer. The screen now carries the inscription: On the Barricades.*

CLIVE: [*Whispering excitedly*] It's Max Brown! [*Snaps a photo*]

SALLY: It can't be!

CLIVE: [*Approaching closer to* MAX] It is, Sally, it is.
SALLY: How did he get across the frontier –
CLIVE: Past the police of seven countries –
SALLY: So sure of himself. So strong.
CLIVE: Go on, Sally, you must!
SALLY: I can't. He's so remote; so formidable.
CLIVE: [*Pushing her forward*] Go on, it will make you!
SALLY: [*Close to* MAX] Max Brown . . .
MAX: [*Remote, not looking at her*] Well?
SALLY: [*Clinging to him*] Oh Max, oh Max.
CLIVE: [*Snapping photos, writhing about like an eel*] Marvellous, marvellous! More thigh, darling, more, more!

SALLY *and* CLIVE *slip into the crowd. The militants take a step forward.* MAX *is now their leader. His head turns upwards. He is spotlit. His voice is at first dreamy, but soon bolder and more confident.*

MAX: Max Brown . . . iron-willed disciple of Marx and Bakunin, the self-effacing yet unchallenged leader of the movement. Men follow him spontaneously, women compete to satisfy his needs. [MAX *and his followers abruptly change posture.*] Paris! Max Brown arrives secretly in Paris with his hair dyed red and things begin to move. The paving stones come up and the poplars come down on the Boul Mich. Max is in the front line, speaking perfect French, deploying his city guerrillas against the CRS, scattering before the tear gas, cunningly regrouping on the Right Bank, converging on the Senate. [*A cry from the militants who now lift* MAX *on to their shoulders*] The bankers panic, the Bourse is in flames, workers' councils spring up, spontaneous and democratic. The regime totters . . . falls . . . totters. Max Brown is now the supreme leader of a movement without leaders. He is interviewed by Jean-Paul Sartre. In your presence, says the great philosopher, I must learn everything afresh.

End of Tableau. The militants disperse to the sides. MAX *remains alone, somewhat stunned. He is confronted now by* MARKO, *a rich and shambling hippie, who shuffles around him.*

MARKO: Did two beautiful people come this way? [*Pause*] Man, I'm stiff. Where's the john? [*Pause*] Did you ever see so many sado-mas. suffragettes and pot crazy babies? [*Pause*] This daylight's a torment, don't you think? This whole protest thing is a middle-class fake-in. I'm dry. [*Pause*] Did someone dwarf your psyche? Do you have a political hang-up or something? [*Pause*] Do you need acid? [*Pause. He drifts away*] Groovy talking to you.

The screen now carries the inscription: *The Workers.* ANN *approaches four youths.*

ANN: [*Offering leaflets*] Join the struggle against war and imperialism.

1ST YOUTH: War and who?

3RD YOUTH: What's it got to do with you?

ANN: It's the concern of all of us. It's our duty to bring pressure on the Government.

1ST YOUTH: [*Grinning*] I know where I'd like to bring pressure.

They form a circle round her.

2ND YOUTH: Ever been had?

4TH YOUTH: She talks very posh and all.

ANN: Don't you know how many people are being killed every day?

3RD YOUTH: Yeah, on the roads. Come on, give us a breath test. [*The others hold him back*]

ANN: Couldn't you spare just one afternoon to help the women and children of Vietnam?

3RD YOUTH: I could spare an evening. Where do we meet?

4TH YOUTH: She needs a good knock-up. Bert's the one for that.
1ST YOUTH: She'd never stop talking from start to finish.
3RD YOUTH: She'd come to the point and I'd be a Vietcong.
ANN: [*Attempting to break away*] Excuse me.
3RD YOUTH: A bird with education is a flea in your pants.
1ST YOUTH: Go on, get lost.

They push her away roughly. She runs into the crowd. The YOUTHS *saunter off.* BRIGHT *walks on stage, surveys the scene with evident satisfaction. When he snaps his fingers the image of Trafalgar Square vanishes from the screen. We shall soon see why. The crowd now draws back and* BRIGHT *exits. All attention is now directed to a* YOUNG VIETNAMESE WOMAN *and her small* BROTHER, *who stands beside her. He is mutilated. Near by stands a man, a* WITNESS, *holding a cluster of photographs. Whenever he shows one of these it appears on the screen, magnified. The crowd is quiet. But first the screen carries the inscription: A Moving Episode.*

YOUNG WOMAN: I am twenty-four years old and I have two brothers and two sisters.

The WITNESS *shows a photograph of the assembled family.*

I live in Quanghanh in Quanglinh Province. I am a schoolteacher.

The WITNESS *shows a photograph of the young woman with her class outside the schoolhouse.*

Quanghanh is a small village
Far away
Very far away
From any factory, railway
Or soldiers' camp.
Far also
From any electricity generating plant.

On every side of our village
Are ricefields.
The planes come regularly in daytime.
Always from the same direction
A distant droning like bees,
Yet heavier.
The planes come low
They circle slowly over our village
Choosing their target.

The witness shows a photograph of an American bomber.

After the first attack
Or the second
They climb away
Making a great noise
But not before the first-aid post too
Has been destroyed.

The WITNESS *shows a photograph of bamboo huts destroyed.*

A pellet lodged in my brain.
They say it is lodged too deep to remove.

The WITNESS *shows an X-ray photograph of her brain.*

I can no longer see clearly.
The world about me is blurred and restless
As if I were underwater.
I have severe headaches
Sometimes so severe
That I am led to scream and roll upon the ground
Like a madwoman.
Changes of temperature
Are particularly to be feared.
Such a person must of course
Continue to teach.
My small pupils are most kind
And crowd around me in my distress

And attempt to take my head
In their hands.

The WITNESS *shows once again the photograph of the young woman with her pupils outside the schoolhouse.*

Do here is my brother by adoption.
His father and mother and two uncles
Died from napalm burns.
In June last year Do and three other boys
Were herding buffalo.

The WITNESS *shows a photograph of the boy with buffalo.*

It was midday and the sun
Was high,
The plane too was high up.

The WITNESS *shows a photograph of an American bomber.*

The plane circled the field.
It came lower.
The boys began to run
The buffaloes to stampede.

The WITNESS *shows the photographs of the bomber and the boy with buffalo in rapid succession.*

The plane became silent
As if
The engines had been switched off.
My brother remembers only the sound of his own breath
And the shadow of the plane.

The WITNESS *shows a photograph of the* BOY *lying on a hospital bed, burned and mutilated. The crowd close sympathetically round the* YOUNG WOMAN *and* BOY, *and then leave the stage. An* AMERICAN BYSTANDER *buttonholes* TOM, FRANK, MAX *and* ANN.

AMERICAN: What do you make of that?

TOM: Make of it?

AMERICAN: It's just a repeat performance of the Stockholm Tribunal. Kind of a travelling road show. Reminds me of *Alice in Wonderland* – you know, the children's tale. The sentence came first and the trial afterwards.

FRANK: I doubt whether the book was intended for children.

AMERICAN: It's a pity they don't show photos of what the VC do to their own people. [*At this* FRANK, TOM *and* MAX *close in on him*] The kids in the States aren't concerned with realities anymore. They just sit around Central Park burning their draft cards.

They are abruptly bathed in green light. Henceforward all physical movements take place in stylised slow motion.

MAX: Better than burning villages, isn't it?

AMERICAN: Of course you know who's behind all this. In my opinion it's tragic to watch a great scholar degenerate into a totem pole of extremism. [MAX, FRANK *and* TOM *now begin to beat and kick the* AMERICAN. *As he crawls off stage he continues to talk and they continue to kick him.*] He's nothing but a sounding board for Communist drum beats, the decrepit figurehead of a movement composed of ambitious nonentities who make a big-time career out of protest.

The stage is empty.

SCENE TEN

The hallway of the students' union. A RECRUITING OFFICER *sits behind a table and beside a large Royal Navy poster. He is bored but confident. Enter* MAX, FRANK *and* TOM, *marching in step. They halt in front of the table, stamping their feet.*

MAX: Sir!

FRANK: Sir!

MAX: Permission to sail into the 1970's –

FRANK: Small but strong –

TOM: Rapidly deployed –

MAX: Invisible and invincible. The hidden dissuader.

FRANK: What you need is a new type of officer, the man with a degree and a Midland Bank account, the trend-setting young executive in blue.

TOM: That's us.

MAX: Just in case any foreigners try anything on –

TOM: We have them and they have them.

MAX: We deter them but they don't deter us –

FRANK: From using ours second if they use theirs first.

MAX: Because we, second to none, invincible and invisible –

TOM: Are ever-ready to make a preventive strike –

FRANK: To paralyse their capability to paralyse our capability –

MAX: To keep them guessing.

FRANK: And if they guess wrong –

TOM: We burn them to cinders.

ALL THREE: Sir! [*They salute*]

With a concerted movement, they overturn the table, seize the officer, and drag him away by the legs.

SCENE ELEVEN

The University: The office of Hugh Garfield. GARFIELD, MAX, ANN, MAY, FRANK, TOM. HUGH GARFIELD, *thirty-five years old, is lecturer in Political Science. His personality, which lacks charm, suggests an ambiguous ambition. On the walls of his office hang pictures of Lenin, Trotsky, Guevara – and the Beatles. Plus a Vietcong flag.*

GARFIELD: [*Distributing cans of beer*] The best thing about America was the ice-box in my office.

ANN: I didn't know you had been in the States.

GARFIELD: I thought I might do some good there. There's always a limited room for manoeuvre under neo-facism. Also the salary was hard to turn down. I was thrown out after six months.

ANN: Out of America or out of the university?

GARFIELD: It comes to the same thing. You can't stay if you can't get work.

MAX: What happened?

GARFIELD: I was accused of encouraging students to evade the draft. They found out I was organising an emigration network.

ANN: Were you followed by the FBI?

GARFIELD: My phone was tapped. Incidentally, I approve the collective stand you girls have taken. The administration is very shaken-up by it. Mind you, Ann, your political science grades haven't been so hot recently. Mostly B's and C's. [*He leans over her*] So I gave you B's and A's.

ANN: That's hardly fair on the others.

GARFIELD: I'm certainly not going to penalise you for your political activities. Besides – you have nice legs.

The STUDENTS *are embarrassed.*

ANN: Well, what do we do next?

FRANK: There's no alternative now between capitulation and pushing ahead.

MAY: But what does pushing ahead mean?

FRANK: It means revolution.

GARFIELD: I think that's right. We have to escalate rapidly.

ANN: Can we beat the system in the long run? The system is octopus-like; each tentacle germinates eight others.

TOM: The problem is clearly posed: student power or not.

GARFIELD: A revolution is a continuous process of pressure which finally produces a qualitative change in the system. Demands and more demands. But the demands are means, not ends.

ANN: People talk about student power. I suppose I would agree with it if only I knew what it meant.

TOM: We can't sit here and decide what it means. The outcome will be determined by the mass of students in the course of the struggle.

GARFIELD: What we have to consider now is strategy. We have to demonstrate that illegal tactics are effective, and that the administration is as vulnerable as an old tramp ship with a hole in its side caught in a storm. I believe that the majority of students here are completely fed up, but they lack confidence in their own power.

MAX: How do we convince them?

GARFIELD: By bringing the system to a standstill. By closing down official classes and starting our own. By boycotting the exams. That's crucial. Exams are only two weeks away. They are the pivot of the University's value-structure. They are also its functional link with the wider system outside.

ANN: I suppose some students do want to take their exams. We have to be fair to them.

GARFIELD: Stop saying 'fair', Ann. Lenin never used the word. Exams and degrees are the student's passport to a place in the elitist superstructure. We have to free the students from their own fears and ambitions.

MAX: Force them to be free?

GARFIELD: Precisely. But don't quote Rousseau too often. It can lead to petty-bourgeois deviations.

ANN: People often say that the University is merely a part

of the whole repressive system. I keep talking to people who ask: how can you hope to change a part without changing the whole?

FRANK: Tell them we have to start somewhere, and the best place to start is your own doorstep.

TOM: In the long run, the support of the working class will prove decisive.

GARFIELD: Yes, but first we have to have something to show them. The workers take a cool view of student hot-heads, *fils à papa*, as they say in France, who shoot their mouths off until daddy buys them a motor car. We have to change that image.

MAX: I suppose you know that the Great White Enoch himself is due to speak at to the Conservative Association tomorrow. [*Parodies Enoch*]. 'In my opinion, and all the statistics confirm this, it is in certain concentrated areas that the virtue of our womenfolk is most imperilled.'

MAY: Some of the girls are planning a demonstration.

GARFIELD: Good but not sufficient. We'll have to break the meeting up.

ANN: A lot of students believe in freedom of speech.

GARFIELD: The pattern you established with the Naval Recruiting Officer has to grow and expand. To stand still now is to turn back. What is needed is a kind of disorder which is not the same as chaos – an open field of possibilities which encourages self-assertion and self-rule.

FRANK: The rumour is that the President will bring the police in.

GARFIELD: Let him.

MAX: How many members of the faculty can we count on?

GARFIELD: About five now. If you go places, others will jump on the bandwagon. People like your respected Professor of Drama.

ANN: I'm sure Steven is really on our side.

MAY: He's completely sincere. I mean . . .

GARFIELD: Bright enjoys a fine international reputation.

You can suck the titles of his books and articles like chocolates: 'Revolutionary Theatre'; 'Dialogue as Dialectic'; 'Alienation and Commitment'; 'The Actor as Rebel.' Marvellous.

ANN: I agree he can be absolutely maddening at times, but it's hard not to trust him.

GARFIELD: When Bright talks about life he means art, and when he talks about art he means Bright.

MAX: But he carries a lot of weight with the progressive members of the faculty.

GARFIELD: Naturally. Because he has a foot in both camps. In Boston he gave a lecture to the effect that a writer's best revolutionary weapon was his art – only in exceptional circumstances should he take to the barricades. But for Bright circumstances are never sufficiently exceptional. In any case, the only kind of barricade he knows is a fence. We had this petition about political prisoners in Spain. We asked him to sign it. He said it was badly worded. Badly worded!

Silence.

MAX: Do you propose that we go ahead without him?

GARFIELD: You have no alternative. If Lenin had waited for the Mensheviks, Kerensky would still be in power.

ANN: I think we ought to talk to him at least.

GARFIELD: You'll still be talking when the term ends.

SCENE 12

The stage of the University theatre. BRIGHT *is sitting alone on the stage, surrounded by his personal notes, manuscripts and photographs. Enter* MAX, ANN, MAY, FRANK *and* TOM.

BRIGHT: [*Briefly glancing up*] Ah, approach Brutus, Cassius . . . [*Showing them a photograph.*] This is Helene Weigel as Mother Courage, the first time she ever played the part. [*Pause*] Every six months I wade into this debris and wade out again. Occasionally I have a nightmare – that it has all gone up in flames.

ANN: We want to talk to you, Steven.

BRIGHT: About your play? Why did no one turn up for rehearsals yesterday? [*Pause*] I hear that some of you have been trampling on the flag. [*Rummaging through his notes.*] Sartre and Camus quarrelling here . . . 1952, before your time. Of course they were both right. Then Camus died and seized the moral advantage. That's why Sartre felt compelled to turn down the Nobel Prize – because Camus had already taken it with him into the realm of pure freedom.

TOM: Will you support the revolution?

BRIGHT: [*Vaguely searching for a pen*] Where do I sign?

FRANK: Hugh Garfield warned us you would prevaricate.

BRIGHT: Did he? Tell me, will Garfield be Minister of the Interior in your Free University?

MAY: I don't awfully like Hugh. I mean, he sort of insinuates . . .

BRIGHT: What I regard as decent behaviour he calls bourgeois sentimentality. [*Casually*] Can't think why you put him in.

MAX: Put him in what?

BRIGHT: In your play. Mind you, I'm not complaining. I take it to be a sign of your growing maturity as actors, your sense of the complexity of life. Whereas your portrait of me –

MAX: Here we go. Garfield is not in our play. Nor are you.

BRIGHT: [*Jumping up*] Ah! Very subtle. [*Strides about*] Yes, yes, a stroke of genius.

ANN: What is?

BRIGHT: First you artificially create a dramatic pattern of events to bring conviction to your play. Then when I kick up a fuss about banal naturalism, you disarm me by insisting that you are simply students visiting the University theatre. Therefore everything, including what is happening at this moment on this stage, is held to be real – and not part of a play at all.

By this MAX, ANN *and* MAY *are stunned and incredulous. Whereas* FRANK *and* TOM *are impatient.*

FRANK: [*Scornfully*] Precisely. We have to devote all our energies to the revolution.

TOM: [*Moving to the exit*] Which you clearly have no interest in supporting.

ANN: [*Stopping them*] No, no. [*To* BRIGHT] We need the support of people like you.

BRIGHT: Why? If I persuaded the President to give you all a second chance – which I doubt – your revolution would vanish by default. And if, on the contrary, I personally lead the attack on the Bastille, it will be my revolution not yours. [*Pause*] At this moment you are not quite sure of yourselves. But wait until you have set up your Committee of Public Safety in the President's Office. I will be the ideal candidate for the fate of Danton.

MAY: Oh Steven!

BRIGHT: [*Changing mood*] If I do collaborate there is, I suppose, some faint hope of averting a complete artistic shambles. If I stand aside, you will ignore the proper laws and limitations of the stage, there will be endless brawls, real corpses and tear gas thrown into the audience.

MAX: You know perfectly well what we're talking about. This revolution has no script and no director; it embraces the whole University – and beyond.

BRIGHT: Spontaneous theatre, in effect. Sensational, violent, alcoholic. [*Pause*] What happens if I don't collaborate?

FRANK: We can't afford to be sentimental.

BRIGHT: The voice of the true Jacobin. Those who are not with us . . .

TOM: It would be difficult for us to guarantee the physical immunity of this theatre.

BRIGHT: [*Lightly, almost dismissively*] Yes, I can visualise it: camp beds, primus stoves, toilet rolls, stretchers and Chinese spaghetti tins everywhere. Plus an invasion of rats and Katanga mercenaries. Costumes, scenery, equipment ruined.

MAX: It could happen.

Silence. BRIGHT *is stunned. Then he appears to recover himself, adopting the style of a villain in a melodrama.*

BRIGHT: Why, my young friends, it was only my little joke, no? You can always count on the unswerving devotion of your Steven.

FRANK: We'll see.

TOM: Tomorrow the Enoch is due to rant and rave in the Assembly Hall. We intend to break the meeting up.

BRIGHT: I have a certain old-fashioned affection for free speech.

MAX: We prefer freedom. Anyway, as Hugh Garfield says, to stand still now is to turn back. The Dean will retaliate. We will counter-demonstrate. After that it's civil war. It's either them or us.

FRANK: Either they rule or we rule.

MAX: I hope we've made ourselves clear.

The STUDENTS *depart.* BRIGHT *is left alone, confused and distracted.*

BRIGHT: [*To himself*] Us or them . . . Who is us and who is them? [*Pauses*] Does one choose or is one chosen? [*Pauses then laughs*] It could be quite funny . . . an extravaganza, with the entire Administration of the University barricaded inside the President's offices. [*As* BRIGHT *speaks the next scene is clearly being set up in the background.*] The

Assistant Dean behaving like a cowboy in a mortar board. [BRIGHT *now produces a text bound in bright red. Is it the text of the students' play or the text of this play?*] The text, the text. [*Turning pages.*] That'a right, scene twelve, the students deliver an ultimatum to Bright who pretends to give way. He pretends to believe that the theatrical illusion is a reality. Scene thirteen, the President's office...

SCENE THIRTEEN

The office of the President of the University. PRESIDENT, DEAN, ASSISTANT DEAN, WOMEN'S DEAN, *two* BODYGUARDS. *The* PRESIDENT *is seated behind his desk. The* DEAN, *in gown and mortar board, stands at his side. The* ASSISTANT DEAN, *similarly attired, and carrying a rifle, peers cautiously out of the window. Silence. Then the sound of chopping, outside.*

PRESIDENT: What is that noise?

ASSISTANT DEAN: They're chopping down the poplars in the courtyard, sir.

PRESIDENT: Why?

DEAN: Mr President, he's not obliged to know why. The situation is most unusual. We – that is to say, you – really must expedite decisive action.

ASSISTANT DEAN: Battering rams.

PRESIDENT: What?

ASSISTANT DEAN: They're making battering rams.

PRESIDENT: Isn't occupying the lecture rooms, the library, the refectory, the gymnasium and whatever else we have, enough for them? Do they intend to go beyond passive resistance?

Burst of machine gun fire outside.

DEAN: Evidently.

ASSISTANT DEAN: I wouldn't put much faith in their anti-aircraft guns, but their tanks seem to be in pretty good shape.

PRESIDENT: There was no mention of this kind of thing at the last conference of university presidents and vice-chancellors.

DEAN: We must call in the police.

The WOMEN'S DEAN *faints. They revive her.*

WOMEN'S DEAN: [*Reviving*] Seventy girls dishonoured. And now this. Is there – an orgy out there?

ASSISTANT DEAN: Well – the revolutionary art students seem to be pretty busy covering your girls with luminous paint, tattoos and that sort of thing.

WOMEN'S DEAN: Their clothes will be ruined.

ASSISTANT DEAN: They're no longer wearing clothes.

DEAN: We must call in the police.

PRESIDENT: Do stop saying that! Have you no sense of history? Do you not recall the blunders, provocations and precipitate over-reactions which have been the undoing of countless well-intentioned chief executives, from Louis XVI to Kerensky, Batista and the Presidents of two hundred American universities? Do you imagine that I, a man of broad culture, am going to be trapped into taking action?

ASSISTANT DEAN: If you won't call in the police, sir, there is one other solution. [*He exits*]

PRESIDENT: No! Not that!

WOMEN'S DEAN: Good heavens! Not what?

PRESIDENT: I've seen his shelves crammed with whipping, spanking and bondage books.

The ASSISTANT DEAN *returns with the* CAPTAIN OF RUGBY, *attired in rugger kit, and the* CAPTAIN OF ROWING, *carrying an oar. General astonishment.*

ASSISTANT DEAN: I had in mind the tactics employed by Alexander the Great during the Persian wars. The rowing eight go in first. You can cleave a man in two with an oar, if you know how to use it. If you keep your head, he'll lose his. Then the first fifteen go round the blind side on a kick-and-rush basis to secure the rout. Speak, Bagley of Eton.

CAPT. OF RUGBY: Well, sir, it's simple. First you break them up into small groups. Then you break them up into smaller groups. Then you just break them up.

PRESIDENT: [*Wringing his hands*] No! Say no more. Send them back to the Crown and Anchor. I intend to handle this crisis in a model fashion. *Exit the* CAPTAIN OF RUGBY *and the* CAPTAIN OF ROWING.

The PRESIDENT *rises to his feet.* For what, after all, is the essence of academe, the crystal shrine, the altar of learning which no iconoclast can smash, this Platonic symposium, this museum of the future, this seminary of reason and superstition, this bare ceiling awaiting its Raphael, this upturned telescope awaiting its young Galileo . . .

While he is speaking the ASSISTANT DEAN *has begun to fire a rifle from the window. He reels back coughing and closes the window.*

ASSISTANT DEAN: Tear gas.

DEAN: Wait a minute – tear gas is supposed to be our thing, not theirs.

ASSISTANT DEAN: Nothing for it, we'll have to make molotov cocktails. [*To the* PRESIDENT] Do you have any old whisky bottles?

The telephone goes. ASSISTANT DEAN *answers it.*

PRESIDENT: Well?

ASSISTANT DEAN: Someone in the Government. They want to know what would be most useful: an air-sea rescue operation by Coastal Command, a pay and productivity agreement, a Royal Commission, or the cutting off of all supplies except essential supplies.

PRESIDENT: Hopeless. Summon Professor Bright. He must mediate.

ASSISTANT DEAN: [*Picking up the telephone*] Bright – come over here at once. [*Pause*] What? No, I can't guarantee you covering fire.

At once the door opens and BRIGHT *enters.*

DEAN: You were remarkably quick.

BRIGHT: I know the text.

PRESIDENT: [*Outraged*] Professor Bright, you are paunchy, self-satisfied, well-paid and entitled to half-price wine in the Senior Common Room. In other words, you are one of us. Yet I observe that your theatre has not been invaded by the enraged mob. Very suspicious. I smell a dirty deal somewhere. You, sir, are the snake in the grass!

BRIGHT: I am merely the grass in the snake.

PRESIDENT: What is to be done?

BRIGHT: Stop fooling about.

DEAN: That's no way to address the President.

BRIGHT: You're overdoing it. I agreed to collaborate with you –

DEAN: With us, you say! With them, you mean –

BRIGHT: With *you*. On condition that I exerted some small influence. [*He coughs*] And I warned you not to use real tear gas. Anyway, the President isn't the drooling idiot you make him out to be.

PRESIDENT: Yes he is – I am.

BRIGHT: The Assistant Dean is sinister enough without his library being stocked with sado-mas.

ASSISTANT DEAN: [*Enormously extravagant*] Ha! I'll pull your balls off, Bright – *slowly*. [*He subsides*]

Silence

BRIGHT: All I ask is this: don't overdo it.

Silence again.
The mood becomes sober.

PRESIDENT: The problem is essentially this: do we negotiate with the self-styled Student Co-ordinating Committee, or do we stand on our rights?

DEAN: To negotiate with the Committee is to recognise its existence.

WOMEN'S DEAN: What exists becomes in the course of time legitimate.

DEAN: There is no evidence that the Committee is representative of student opinion as a whole.

ASSISTANT DEAN: If we meet one demand, they will produce another. Then another. We'll end up by giving them our trousers.

BRIGHT: You're being optimistic.

PRESIDENT: I have in front of me a document circulated by the Student Co-ordinating Committee. It begins with a general onslaught on all forms of entrance examination, which it describes as pernicious reflections of class distinctions. Then come two remarkable theses. Thesis one: The proper function of university students is to subvert the system which alienates and suppresses them. Thesis two: It is the duty of Society to subsidise the University and to provide its students with all necessary facilities for political activity. [*Pause*] Professor Bright.

BRIGHT: Yes, Mr President.

PRESIDENT: Do you subscribe to the content of this manifesto?

BRIGHT: I have never found myself in complete agreement with anything that I did not write myself. And even then, only rarely.

PRESIDENT: I have invited you here in the hope that you might provide a bridge between the philosophy of the militant students and our own.

BRIGHT: Not being in agreement with either, I am a bad candidate.

PRESIDENT: At least you are not one of the ten members of the faculty who have pledged their unconditional support to the students. Did I, in your opinion, have any alternative but to suspend them from their duties?

BRIGHT: A mouse cannot usefully interpret the moral duty of a cat.

PRESIDENT: [*Growing hostile*] It is surely no coincidence that the University theatre has not yet been occupied?

BRIGHT: Would you like to see it sacked?

DEAN: Professor Bright, there is a strong school of thought, to which I confess I belong, which lays the balance of responsibility for this fiasco at your door – perhaps I should say at your stage door. Is it not the case that in recent days you have been rehearsing some form of dramatic exercise based on a students' revolt?

BRIGHT: Every sensible Englishman knows that art is merely a diversion. Sometimes it has a therapeutic value.

PRESIDENT: So your intention was to divert resentments and aggressive tendencies from the campus itself to the stage? You really ask us to believe that?

BRIGHT: Yes.

PRESIDENT: Is that what you tell your students?

BRIGHT: No.

Silence.

DEAN: I don't believe that what you do or don't do on stage makes much difference. The serious charge against you is general permissiveness. Grades, for example. You give all your students Grade A.

BRIGHT: Only those I retain. I encourage on average eighty per cent of my students to withdraw from the Drama School.

DEAN: But those who stay all get A's. Now this is the time-bomb you have planted under our feet.

WOMEN'S DEAN: If they are assured of getting A's, why should they work? Why should they learn their lines or attend rehearsals?

BRIGHT: Sometimes they don't.

ASSISTANT DEAN: I suppose they spend their afternoons happily copulating.

BRIGHT: The ability to be happy in that activity must surely be the envy of everyone in this room.

PRESIDENT: But we have an obligation to provide incentives for greater effort. An obligation to society, which subsidises us; an obligation to the candidates we reluctantly turn away.

BRIGHT: I am not inclined to view all human activities as alternatives: work or play; manual labour or protected study. This puritanical respect for grades is part of a system which sets human nature against itself, a system by which men exploit, manipulate and rule other men. A system by which a class preserves the skills which ensure its dominant position.

WOMEN'S DEAN: But they have grades in Russia.

BRIGHT: Precisely.

PRESIDENT: I have never been conscious of such thoughts.

BRIGHT: A man has the subconscious he deserves.

DEAN: But how can any institution survive without rules and sanctions to enforce them?

BRIGHT: Perhaps it depends on who makes the rules, and how adaptable they are to human needs. The best rules are usually made by the people who have to observe them.

DEAN: I suppose there is room for one utopian in every university. Obviously the irredeemable delinquent does not figure in your vision of the world.

BRIGHT: It occurs to me that you are making irredeemable delinquents out of our most intelligent and sensitive students.

Silence.

PRESIDENT: Hm. Well. Bickering and recriminations won't help now. No doubt we have made mistakes. [*To* BRIGHT] What would you advise?

BRIGHT: Advise?

PRESIDENT: What in hell's name should we do now?

BRIGHT: I am a yogi not a commissar.

PRESIDENT: Surely you agree that the student rebels can be divided into maximalists and minimalists?

DEAN: Very shrewd, Mr President.

PRESIDENT: Yes, but what then?

BRIGHT: I don't know. I suppose you could close the University, re-open it, then close it again. [*Pause*] Then re-open it.

PRESIDENT: [*Shouting*] Please be serious! Time is not on our side. In my opinion you are the man to speak to the students. They trust you. You must assure them that we fully recognise the need for reform. Suggest a commission of inquiry. More participation.

BRIGHT: Do you know how the students conjugate the word 'participate'? It goes like this: I participate, you participate, he or she participates, they rule.

DEAN: Most amusing.

BRIGHT: So you want me to advise them to abandon the struggle?

PRESIDENT: Advise them to see reason: to evacuate the buildings, resume normal classes – and respect the rules.

BRIGHT: A complete sell-out. And if I refuse?

PRESIDENT: [*Extravagantly ferocious*] I shall judge your attitude to be one of complicity with the rebellion. Your refusal to denounce violence will be taken as an implicit endorsement of violence. And I shall not find it difficult to present this implicit endorsement as explicit incitement to violence. You will therefore be held unworthy of your position of academic responsibility. I shall suspend you from your duties. There will be protests. I, supported by all the businessmen, bankers, politicians and other disinterested parties who sit on our Council will overrule all protests. A commission of inquiry, handpicked by myself, will investigate my decision. It will confirm my decision. You will be hounded out, persecuted –

DEAN, ASSISTANT DEAN, WOMEN'S DEAN: Yes, yes, hounded out!

Silence.

BRIGHT: Nonsense.

DEAN: Why nonsense?

BRIGHT: Because I give in. I'm your man.

DEAN, ASSISTANT DEAN, WOMAN'S DEAN: You're what!

PRESIDENT: You refuse to make a stand on principle?

BRIGHT: If you threaten me, yes. I refer you to Brecht's Galileo.

WOMEN'S DEAN: But you promised to collaborate with us.

BRIGHT: That's what I'm doing.

DEAN: No, no, with *us*.

PRESIDENT: You are not playing your part.

BRIGHT: On the contrary, it is you who are misunderstanding yours. Usual vice: excessive naturalism leading to grotesque exaggeration. I wish you could see yourselves. I ask you: is it really probable that a sane President would sack a Professor for *refusing* to make a speech?

PRESIDENT: Then what? How do we get out of this?

BRIGHT: How do you advance the action? Easy. Immediate violence. Unleash yourselves upon yourselves. Holocaust.

PRESIDENT: Ah. Yes. You mean we can expect an immediate physical assault on this building?

BRIGHT: Very immediate.

PRESIDENT: [*Resuming his role*] A physical attack! Outrageous!

DEAN, ASSISTANT DEAN, WOMEN'S DEAN: Scandalous! Barbaric!

Footsteps, shouts outside. The door bursts open. Enter GARFIELD, MAX, FRANK, TOM *and other* STUDENTS.

MAX: There are more outside. We advise you not to resist. We mean business.

BRIGHT: [*Aside*] What an appalling line.

FRANK *and* TOM *eject the* PRESIDENT *from his chair. The authorities are overpowered.* GARFIELD *motions to* MAX, *who now occupies the President's chair. On the screen a portrait of Macmillan in academic robes, which has been there from the beginning, is instantly replaced by one of Guevara.* GARFIELD *offers* MAX *one of the President's cigars, and lights it for him.* MAX *picks up a document lying on the President's desk.*

MAX: [*Reading*] Case of Max Brown. The Senate, acting on the advice of the President, and in the light of evidence submitted by the Dean, and having conferred with the Disciplinary Sub-Committee of Convocation is unanimously resolved that the said Max Brown be convicted of irredeemable delinquency and therefore hung by the neck until dead. [*He tears up the document*]

PRESIDENT: I wish to speak.

GARFIELD: Too bad.

MAX: Speak.

PRESIDENT: No doubt you think of yourselves as idealists, In reality you are adolescents and [*indicating* GARFIELD] honorary adolescents having a temper tantrum. You have entered now the infernal cycle of violence from which there is no escape. The hands laid on me were the hands which laid the foundation stone of your concentration camps. That is all.

MAX: Take these gentlemen to the Dean's office and keep an eye on them. They may be fed three two-course meals a day. Or two three-course meals. Or one six-course meal. Three gallons of wine per head per day will be enough.

GARFIELD: Bright will no doubt wish to keep his friends company.

MAX: [*To* BRIGHT] What do you think – Professor?

BRIGHT: I think that the melodrama is infectious – even among actors who look forward to careers in the serious theatre. I also observe a hole in the sole of your shoe.

MAX *hesitates, half removes his foot from the desk. But a small gesture from* GARFIELD *prompts him to replace his foot. As he blows cigar smoke, the words 'student power' appear on the screen.*

Act Two

SCENE ONE

The University theatre. A large and animated general assembly of STUDENTS *is congregating. Banners and slogans abound – boycott exams: to be young is to be alive: drop outs drop in: learn to live, live to learn, etc. A hotplate has been installed, and then first aid gear.*

Where a line is attributed to 'a student' or to 'a voice', it should not be spoken by any named character. The tendency should be resisted to restrict the lines to a few, familiar faces. The play is at this point moving from the dramatic to the epic – consequently the effect must be one of surging mass activity and participation. The greatest danger is that the words will get lost in a general rhubarb of noise. Or, alternatively, that the eye will be satiated at the expense of the ear. In general improvisation should be avoided.

MAX: We have to awaken . . . we have to awaken by an effective dialectic of mass action . . . the radicalism of the wage-earning masses.

FRANK: We must think in terms of a long march through the institutions. One edifice will crack after another. Every contradiction must be exposed and deepened.

A STUDENT: Power lies in the streets. Build barricades, fight the police, burn down the stock exchange.

MAX: Maybe. But don't let's wage war against symbols.

A VOICE: What about the political parties?

A VOICE: Destroy them. They're all parties of fear.

A STUDENT: That's fine. But shouldn't we be discussing what we're going to do here?

MAX: We have appealed to all progressive members of the faculty to co-operate with us.

A VOICE: We don't need them.

MAX: I believe we do. They have knowledge and skills we don't have.

A VOICE: The wrong knowledge and the wrong skills.

A STUDENT: Okay, you've told us who's in the team. So what game are we going to play?

A STUDENT: Blueprints are fatal. Just let the thing develop.

A STUDENT: Deal with each problem as it comes up.

A STUDENT: The first thing is to make contact with the workers. The working class alone has the power to overthrow the system. All this talk about institutions is a petty-bourgeois deviation.

GARFIELD: I disagree with that. As Lenin said, a system cracks at its weakest link. At the present time, the universities are the weakest link in the authoritarian, pseudo-democratic, consumer society. It is in the area of knowledge and communications that the hierarchical structure is most manaced by the rapidity of change. Certainly the students are not the revolutionary class, or a class at all. They are the vital element which deserts from the ruling class. They are the revolutionary catalyst.

A VOICE: That makes sense.

BRIGHT: May I speak?

MAX: Does Professor Bright have the floor?

A VOICE: Ask him what he was doing in the President's office when you arrived. Ask him whether he has a bad conscience.

BRIGHT: [*He speaks with pain and tension.*] I do have a bad conscience. I find it indispensable to creative activity. [*Pause*] I observe something with sadness and consternation. I observe it all around me. I observe you. Good God, why does your headquarters, transit camp, first aid post, assembly hall and general kibbutz have to be my theatre?

VOICES: Our theatre. Our theatre. Our theatre.

BRIGHT: Very well, then, your theatre. Surely you are aware, particularly the drama students among you, of the damage you have already done. You have here the most lavishly equipped and endowed university theatre in the country –

VOICES: Down with equipment!
Down with endowments!
Down with lavish . . .

BRIGHT: I have not deserved this!

VOICES: Out! Out!

BRIGHT: When the President summoned me, I threw my weight behind your cause –

VOICES: Feather weight
Blows in the wind
Out, out, out.

BRIGHT: Let me speak!

VOICES: Out, out.

BRIGHT *leaves angrily. Next to speak is* SHANE, *a large and muscular American student; of whom more later.*

SHANE: Seems to me we still haven't found the first problem.

FRANK: I agree with that. It may be fine to dream of utopia inside the commune, but it's as well to remember that the commune is under fire.

TOM: That's true. We need to work out some form of self-government.

1ST STUDENT: Government is a bad word, man. Anarchy is the only solution.

2ND STUDENT: Down with all dogmas!

1ST STUDENT: Anarchy is against all dogmas.

2ND STUDENT: Against all dogmas except anarchy.

MAX: 'Down with all dogmas' is a dogma.

1ST STUDENT: This whole movement goes back to Bakunin.

Propaganda by deed. That's what it's all about.

SHANE: We all have a sexual hang-up. I'd go for propaganda by seed.

MAX: We already have a Co-ordinating Committee. Should we keep it? If so, should its members be re-elected every day, every week, or what?

A STUDENT: Elections are a form of alienation. Let's keep this thing fluid and spontaneous.

A STUDENT: That only leads in practice to the cult of personality. The rule of people with red hair and blue eyes.

GARFIELD: Let's consider the situation concretely. We have a refectory and a kitchen to run. Food will have to be bought, our garbage won't vanish of its own accord. If we are put under siege, medical facilities will have to be taken care of. I propose that a committee be elected to take responsibility for all this.

MAX: Is that agreed?

VOICES: Agreed.

MAX: Under the chairmanship of Miss Ann Martin, whose organisational talents are a tribute to her sex and indeed to British youth. Agreed?

ANN: Oh no . . .

MAX: Objection over-ruled. That's agreed.

GARFIELD: There is a second kind of committee we ought to consider. Its nature is political rather than administrative.

A VOICE: Power-hungry urchins of the ghettos, arise!

GARFIELD: The question is this: do you restrict this committee to a purely agitational role, or do you delegate to it a measure of real authority?

SHANE: Purely agitational, man. No politburos in the zen of the nuts.

GARFIELD: Tomorrow we may receive a visit from a few hundred policemen. And they won't come to discuss the weather. Does the situation just take care of itself?

A VOICE: Yes, leave it open . . .

SHANE: This guy's got a mile of red tape in his pocket.

GARFIELD: There are plenty of precedents. Is it bourgeois to learn from experience? Is it bourgeois to anticipate events?

A STUDENT: Yes, it is.

The lights are lowered. General movement about the stage indicates passing time. A radio news broadcast is heard.

RADIO: There were violent clashes in London today between police and students. Two hundred police struggled with students in the forecourt of the University. Other police detachments fought a running battle in the streets with demonstrators who threw bricks and tore up paving stones. Many injuries are reported and there was extensive damage to public and private property.

The lights come up. MAX *runs on wearing a policeman's helmet. Cheers.*

MAX: A police inspector arrived with his sturdy satraps and demanded that we release the President. We declined. Quick to recognise the presence of superior force, the inspector withdrew.

FRANK: In the Art School this morning the air is thick with smoke. A number of psychedelic and kinetic geniuses are openly peddling pot. [*Some cheers*]

A STUDENT: For money or not for money?

FRANK: Apparently for love of mankind.

SHANE: Then that's their affair, Herr Hang-Up.

A VOICE: How about the contraceptive machine? When's it going to be set up?

GARFIELD: Let's get back to the pot peddlers. That was never settled. Nothing would please our enemies more than to see us degenerate into a drugged and stupefied rabble.

SHANE: Robespierre constructs his Committee of Public Sanity.

GARFIELD: Have you ever tried fighting the police when you're high?

SHANE: Man, the cops are always high, that's why they win.

A STUDENT: In Vietnam the GI's are soaked in sugar while the VC keep cool on rice and fried worms.

SHANE: Man, a fried worm can turn you higher than the sky.

MAX: Do we prohibit the peddling of pot?

VOICES: No, no . . .

VOICES: Yes, yes.

A VOICE: It is prohibited to prohibit.

MAX: The libertarians prevail for the time being. A more immediate crisis concerns the science and engineering students. They're all working away like beavers.

A STUDENT: They're sick. Science is sick.

A STUDENT: Send an agitation party to talk to them.

FRANK: We did. They said they'd turn us into vegetables and send us into orbit round the moon.

A STUDENT: All they want is three thousand a year, a company car and a weekend cottage in Sussex.

SHANE: Feed them pot.

MAX: A united front of students remains impossible so long as the science students continue to prepare for their exams.

TOM: Cut off their gas, water and electricity for a start.

A STUDENT: Trouble is, they'll make their own.

A STUDENT: Send the girls across with white feathers, like in the first world war.

A STUDENT: Tell them we're having one hell of an orgy over here.

MAX *receives a message.*

MAX: The Ministry of Education want us to send a delegation to talk to them.

VOICES: No. Stay put.

GARFIELD: No delegations, no dialogue, no deals.

A STUDENT: We no longer have demands. This struggle has no objective. It is the objective.

ANN: Surely we ought to formulate some programme.

SHANE: People who formulate never copulate.

A STUDENT: Programmes are divisive.

MAX *receives another message.*

MAX: A message from the television people. They want permission to bring their cameras in here.

A VOICE: No! The medium is the morgue.

GARFIELD: The TV men invented the three D's: distort, distract, denigrate.

VOICES: Let them come, what are you afraid of...

The radio and general movement again indicate the passing of time.

RADIO: Bow Street Magistrates' Court has remained in continuous session for the past twenty-four hours as a result of further clashes between students and police. The Ministry of Health has denied a student claim that hospitals have been refusing to treat casualties identifiable as students. A number of eyewitnesses confirm that trucks and vans converted by students into ambulances have been stopped by the police and their injured occupants arrested.

TV cameras are brought in. FRANK *and* TOM *arrive with two young* WORKERS.

FRANK: We went to the Conway Motor Corporation and tried to open up a dialogue with the workers.

TOM: The management and the union officials wouldn't let us in. They told us to push off. They called us hot-heads, trouble makers, beatniks and the rest.

FRANK: We went to the Argos Steel Works. The police were waiting. They turned us back.

TOM: Then several of the younger workers pushed their way through the police lines. They wanted to hear what we had to say.

Cheers for the two WORKERS, *who sit down at a table with* FRANK *and* TOM.

FRANK: What shall we discuss?
VOICES: Alienation
Apartheid
Vietnam
De-humanization.
1ST WORKER: Work.
FRANK: We know that you arc exploited. We know that because we also are exploited.
2ND WORKER: The working man lives by overtime and piece-work. Don't talk to me about the forty-hour week. They drive us like donkeys. You wouldn't understand.
TOM: We do understand. We are with you.
1ST WORKER: The work you do isn't work by my way of thinking.
2ND WORKER: Work is hard and long. It pisses you off.
1ST WORKER: All they want is to get the maximum profit out of us. You have to overthrow the system.
FRANK: We agree about that. That's why we have overthrown the system here. But work can become a pleasure when it's dealienated.
1ST WORKER: What does that mean, then?
FRANK: A worker is no longer alienated when he works for himself and his collective, not for a boss.
1ST WORKER: No. Real work is always a grind, always will be. Thing is, under socialism you get less work and more time to yourself.
FRANK: I worked on a collective farm in Cuba. We worked long hours and the sun bit right through your skull. But everyone enjoyed their work, because they were working for themselves and each other.

2ND WORKER: Yeah, but that's a kind of sport, really, isn't it. Building bridges in Yugoslavia and all that. The reason you enjoy sweating it out during your holidays is because you can sit down neat and comfortable the rest of the time. The only time I enjoy myself is when I get away from it all – riding round the countryside on my Norton 650 and laying the girls. I was in the Cotswolds last year, and I put down seven in a week.

TOM: Automation under socialism could change all this.

2ND WORKER: What, laying chicks?

TOM: It could change the nature of the work. Provided it was no longer linked to a system of exploitation.

1ST WORKER: I can't go along with that. Going from the assembly line to automation doesn't make any difference, except a different kind of repetition.

2ND WORKER: And more unemployment.

FRANK: What can we students do to help you?

1ST WORKER: I dunno. The colleges take in mainly the better-off kids. You could maybe make places here for some of us.

TOM: But unless we also change the elitist nature of the University, we'll only be turning more workers into bourgeois.

1ST WORKER: You could leave us to worry about that. Thing is, you see, the workers' experience isn't the same as yours. I mean if you get a load of coppers in here, you can always go some place else. You know you'll land on your feet, see. With us it's different.

The WORKERS *depart. Radio. Passage of time.*

RADIO: The Home Secretary warned the House of Commons today that in future the police may be compelled to resort to tougher methods of law enforcement. Replying to an Opposition question, he confirmed that the tear gas used yesterday outside the University could prove permanently damaging to health. The responsibility, he said, lay with the violent student minority who provoked the disorders. Fifty MP's have signed a petition calling for a revival of National Service, which, they say, would knock some sense into a generation which gets too much for doing too little.

It is night now. Most STUDENTS *lie asleep on the floor. Some are injured.* SHANE *is thumbing through a pile of roneoed sheets, keeping some and rejecting others.*

SHANE: Anarchy. [*Keeps*] Student Power [*Rejects*]. Action, Free Love [*Keeps*]. Mao Speaks [*Rejects*]. Imagination is revolution . . . Every view of things which is not strange is false. [*Keeps*]. The more I make love, the more I make the revolution. [*Keeps*].

The lights go up, it is morning. Two STUDENTS *run in, carrying newspapers.*

1ST STUDENT: Three more universities have fallen to the revolution!

2ND STUDENT: Oxford students form Red Guards and remind the world that in 1917 the Russian workers comprised only two per cent of the population.

MAX: [*Reading from a newspaper*] The Prime Minister announces the following measures to deal with the crisis. The Minister of Education becomes the Minister of Power, the Minister of Power becomes the Minister of Housing, and the Minister of Housing becomes the Minister of Education. The size of the Cabinet is cut from twenty-one to twenty. Ten new peers are created, many of them former Presidents of former universities.

Enter now three visitors from outside: SALLY, CLIVE *and* MARKO.

SALLY: [*Indicating* MAX] There he is! [*Embracing him*] Darling Max, you've been simply heroic. We've seen you on the telly. [CLIVE *snaps photo of their embrace.*]

MARKO: Take a look at some of these crazy posters, man.

SALLY: Those two young workers you found were simply winners. I said to Clive: the proletariat of the dictatorship just has to come. We even left our dinner party early to get here.

CLIVE: [*To* MAX] You've simply no idea what we went through. My dear, the police at the gates are absolute brutes.

ANN: [*To* SALLY *and* CLIVE] For voyeurs, only three guinea seats are available.

CLIVE: [*Confused*] Oh dear. [*Reaches in his pocket*] Would five pounds do?

ANN *laughs and holds up the money. Cheers. Radio and general movement indicate the passing of time.*

RADIO: The Prime Minister said yesterday that although it had not yet proved necessary to employ troops against the students, the situation had deteriorated so far that he could not rule out the possibility. Press comments this morning on the student revolution are increasingly hostile. One editorial remarked, 'If this is what results from higher education, then we can well do without it.'

Enter FRANK *and* TOM, *escorting three distinguished visitors*: JOHN LIGHTFOOT, *well-known leftist journalist,* SAM DOTT, *veteran Communist, and* LEON TIRADE, *veteran Trotskyist.*

FRANK: This is Mr John Lightfoot, editor of the . . . of the . . .

LIGHTFOOT: Of the *New Leader*.

FRANK: Mr Sam Dott of the CP, and Mr Leon Tirade of the SLL. Mr Lightfoot will speak first.

DOTT *and* TIRADE *sit down.*

TV PRODUCER: [*To* LIGHTFOOT] Mr Lightfoot, would you oblige by shifting slightly to your left?

LIGHTFOOT: [*Smoothing his hair*] Of course. [*Smiles*] As long as its to the left. [*Pause. Addresses students.*] First of all, I want to apologise to you for being over twenty-five. [*Deadly silence*] I've brought with me a hundred copies of this week's *New Leader* which you may read free of charge. You will see that in my editorial I have come out one hundred per cent behind all that you have done and all that you stand for.

MAX: [*Aside, to* ANN] Then we may as well pack it in.

LIGHTFOOT: Gone, alas, are the years when we could still dream of an authentic proletarian revolution. The working class in the West is ideologically *déclassé* and psychologically *déraciné*. But what you have given back to us all is *l'espoir*, that *esprit des jeunes* which brings back memories of my own student days at the Sorbonne. Once again I see the young *copains* and *copines* together; once again I smell in the air *les lendemains qui chantent*.

Silence.

MAX: Would anyone care to translate?

LIGHTFOOT: [*Laughing easily*] Do any of you, I wonder, know the French version of the Internationale? In English the lines sound somehow mundane.

DOTT: I'm only a British working man, so you must forgive me if I'm a bit slow to comprehend, but I'd like to ask Mr Lightfoot by what right he presumes to talk about the Internationale. It's a matter of common knowledge that Mr Lightfoot was partaking of the gilded life at Oxford while others of us were risking our lives for Spanish democracy.

TIRADE: You mean you were engaged in the repression of the Spanish revolution and of the international working class.

DOTT: I'd like to explain to these young people that what we had to contend with in Spain were certain groups of saboteurs and provocateurs. Calling themselves revolutionaries, they worked hand in glove with Goebbels and the Gestapo.

TIRADE: With whom your friend Stalin signed a non-aggression pact in 1939.

DOTT: While your friend Trotsky and his minions were sabotaging the building of socialism in the Soviet Union –

TIRADE: By that time a neo-capitalist agglomeration of labour camps controlled by a deformed bureaucracy holding down the working class. You may remember that Lenin once said –

STUDENTS *begin slow handclap.*

DOTT: And I'd remind you of something else Lenin said –

TIRADE: Lenin made it perfectly clear –

Clapping grows louder.

DOTT: Lenin's policy –

VOICES: Enough, enough, enough!

Silence.

LIGHTFOOT: Obsolete Marxist polemics have no interest for young people today. Those of us who remember Abyssinia, the Rhineland crisis, appeasement, Munich, the Nazi-Soviet Pact, the Moscow trials –

VOICES: Enough! Enough!

LIGHTFOOT: [*Losing his temper*] Evidently you think you know everything. Adam and Eve and then the students' revolt. Your ideas aren't as new as many of you apparently believe.

MAX: Do you want us to pay you a copyright fee?

A STUDENT: Go chew the cud of your nostalgia in a field.

A STUDENT: You just tinkle like an ice-cream van.

A STUDENT: When Fidel and his twelve survivors set out to overthrow Batista, they had no programme. For them the revolution itself was the only corridor of experience.

Silence.

FRANK: The revolution isn't something you talk about, it's something you do.

DOTT: [*Furious*] What revolution? Do you refer to this infantile disorder which is taking place here?

VOICES: Close up! Go home! We don't want you.

DOTT: [*Anger rising*] The gilded youth can always play at being Lord Byron or André Malraux. You can amuse yourselves with teach-ins, sit-ins, sleep-ins, strip-ins, love-ins and all the rest, because when these escapades come to an end, you'll continue to inherit the earth. So you ridicule the caution of the workers' organisations, and why? Because you know nothing. You can always set up anti-universities, but when the police or the troops move into Conway Motors, the workers there can't set up an anti-factory.

Silence. DOTT *has made his point.*

VOICES: You are old, old, old. Go to sleep. Throw him out.

FRANK: [*Banging his table*] No, let them speak. We can't talk of freedom in one breath and deny it in the next. No censorship here.

An old, bearded JEW, *with long white hair and a German accent, steps forward out of the crowd.*

OLD JEW: [*Smiling enigmatically*] That would be a great mistake.

Pause.

FRANK: [*Respectfully*] I'm sorry. I don't follow. What would be a great mistake?

OLD JEW: To censor censorship. [*Pause*] What greater tribute can one pay to an idea than to suppress it? We who were alive in Germany thirty years ago do not forget that the road to Auschwitz was paved with words: written words, spoken words. *Juden raus!* Two words, each of them worth three million dead. Now you too are at the beginning of such problems. So you have created a law which forbids incitement to racial hatred. You have learned to defend freedom by curtailing it. Good! So one day I go to a little theatre in Sloane Square. Not to see a play, I am too old for plays, I am no longer capable of suspending my disbelief. No, I go to hear some left-wing gentlemen complaining about censorship. I can understand that they should be indignant when their own plays or those of their friends are censored, but I am amazed to learn that they don't want the plays of their opponents censored either. To a German that sounds very strange. So I stand up in the balcony and I address to these gentlemen a question. Do they or do they not approve of this new law forbidding incitement to racial hatred? It transpires that they do. No one is against the law. A second question, then. Suppose someone writes a play celebrating, yes celebrating, the ovens of Auschwitz. What are they going to do? They call me, for some reason, a red herring. Such a play, they insist, would not last two nights, or even one. I say to them: you are all committed writers. You insist that literature can and should influence men. Yet now you deny it! You stab yourselves in the back! If you maintain that a racist speech can corrupt men, but a racist play cannot, would it not follow that an enlightened speech can enlighten men, but an enlightened play cannot? Well, I have to tell you that these gentlemen remained unmoved by my logic. Apparently the logic of Heidelberg and Auschwitz does not correspond to English logic. So I say to them: do you not appreciate the honour that society accords you when it sends the police to your theatre? What, after all, is more praiseworthy about Soviet Communism than its total intolerence of dissenting writers? The men who silence a Pasternak or a Solzhenitsyn fear Pasternak and Solzhenitsyn because they respect the power of literature. Every time a writer goes to prison, the status of literature in the world is enhanced. What words have the impact and eloquence of the censor's blank page? Only when literature has been totally suppressed will it be totally victorious!

The OLD JEW *smiles benignly and shuffles towards the exit. Silence.*

MAX: [*Moving after the* OLD JEW] I don't know our distinguished visitor's name . . . [*The* OLD JEW *stops and looks at* MAX.] But I would like to ask him why he talks about censorship of literature and drama. What has that got to do with our present situation here?

OLD JEW: You don't know?

MAX: No, I don't.

OLD JEW: Forgive me. I took this meeting . . . all these cameras . . . so vast an audience . . . such peculiar performances . . . to be an act of theatre. Indeed, to be an act of inspired, counter-revolutionary theatre. But forgive me.

As he speaks he removes his hat and beard with a flourish. It is BRIGHT. *He darts away, pursued by a crowd of* STUDENTS. *The lights dim as the stage gradually empties. Radio.*

RADIO: Reports from the University indicate that an apparent threat of a police assault on the North-West area of the campus has led students to transfer their headquarters from the University theatre to the Senate building. Asked whether this change would be permanent, a student spokesman replied that –

MAX: [*The last student to leave, he pauses on his way out.*] – nothing is permanent in a permanent revolution, except the revolution.

SCENE TWO

The University theatre. In luminous colours the screen announces: Anti-University. BRIGHT *has put the University theatre at the disposal of hippies, drop-outs and those students who reject the hard political emphasis of the prevailing student revolutionaries. The Anti-University is partly a product of their enthusiasms and obsessions; but we can also detect in it the maliciously creative hand of* BRIGHT. *He has installed a rope and a set of wall-bars. Throughout the action that follows* BRIGHT *prowls about as silent instigator and observer, taking occasional notes and photographs.* MAY *is breast-feeding her baby and making tea. On the right squats* MARKO, *smoking a pot-pipe, frequently jabbing himself with a needle. Sprawled on the floor beside him is* SALLY, *now bemused and sluttish. Centre-stage,* DAVE DOOLEY, *wild Liverpool poet, is squatting on a lavatory, studying a book.* SHANE, *the American leader of the Anti-University, dressed in judo-kit, is doing Yogi exercises. A group of* STUDENTS *who have enrolled in the Anti-University are attempting with difficulty to assimilate.*

SHANE: [*Continuing his exercises, and speaking in the fragmented manner of Charlie Brown moving from one cartoon box to the next in 'Peanuts'*] We have to be – spontaneous. Which means we have – to be. We have to break right through – have to break – the crust of existence – through to essence.

DOOLEY: [*Looking up from his book, and shifting his position*] Got to let go. That's hard. [*Returns to book*]

SHANE: [*Exercising*] Within four days the Free University had become as unfree as the pre-Free. Bureaucrats – demagogues – despots crazy on words.

MARKO: Words are beans.

DOOLEY: [*Grimacing as he tries to open his bowels*] Ugh! This book is screwball. It purports to be a translation of a nineteenth century Persian work called *One Hundred and Five Postures, Positions and Spiritual Attitudes for Letting Go*. I've tried nine. Could be a long sit-in.

MARKO: He's trying to get underground. But his happening just won't happen.

MAY: Shane.

SHANE: Yes baby?

MAY: I feel repressed. I find all this tolerance repressive.

SHANE: That's right. [*He takes hold of a* STUDENT *and throws him on the mat*] We are deluged in repressive tolerance. [*Throws another* STUDENT] Self-defence for radicals.

DOOLEY: Total de-humanisation.

MAY: My milk's running out.

MARKO: Give the baby pot before it develops multiple schizoid alienation and separation symptoms.

DOOLEY: [*Reading from book*] 'Position 11, commonly used by shivas in South Afghanistan.' What's a bloody shiva? [*Reads*] 'Lower the left buttock so that it revolves in easy limbo above the cavern of the lost spirits.' [*He tries to do this*]

SALLY: [*Drugged*] Give me a happening.

SHANE: [*To the* STUDENTS; *suddenly and inexplicably angry*] Now tune in, bums. Get the picture straight. At the Anti-all distinctions between teachers and students have been eliminated. Is that understood? [*He throws a couple of* STUDENTS, *who lie groaning*] Here there are no authoritarian hang-ups. Here we are all anti-students and anti-teachers, dedicated to employing anti-concepts and anti-words to to creat anti-institutions and destructuralise anti-structures. Is that clear? [*He throws another* STUDENT]

MARKO: It's demystification squared.

DOOLEY: Rub silver ointment into my eyeballs, it says here. Perhaps I ought to eat cabbage. [*To* BRIGHT] Is there anything in that line I'm missing?

SHANE: [*Climbing a rope and swinging to the wallbars*] Only by a radical physical destruction of the conditions which permit and thereby repress dissent . . . [*He breaks off, clings to wallbars*]

SALLY: Will someone ever love me? It's been such a long time since –

MARKO: Time is a bourgeois freak-out. Be your own clock.

DOOLEY: [*Throwing down book*] I've learned sixteen postures and now I'm going to have to anti-learn them.

MARKO: Go underground, man. Like where the Empire State is a mine shaft and then screwing with a girl is like walking into your own head. All you need is a hard-edged burnout to shift your libido into infinity.

A STUDENT: May I ask a question? [*Silence*] I mean, I just wondered about the scene . . . I mean, what goes?

MAY: Shane is on freedom road. That's his scene.

DOOLEY: Sonny boy, it's easy to know the answers to the questions; but I can never remember the questions to the answers. [*He groans*] I feel packed. [*To* BRIGHT] bring me the chamber of terrors. Move, move. [BRIGHT *brings him the tape recorder. He switches on. Sound of muffled voices, space count-down, breaking glass, wrestlers' groans, flushing lavatory, lovers' sighs, Aston's lecture, a road drill, a voice saying 'man of the people', a voice saying 'I'm high', a girl saying 'get in, get in', a voice saying 'sincerely', hysterical laughter, chords of Beethoven. As the tape moves to a climax,* DOOLEY *rolls, stretches and pants on the lavatory. Climaxes in the clatter of falling bricks and the sound of flushing water. He beams with content.*] It's really auto-destructive anti-poetry.

MAY: Why don't you climb off now, Dave?

MARKO: He's waiting for the second coming. He's greedy.

SHANE: What we need is a collective coming. The dialectics of liberation is come, un-come, super-come.

A STUDENT: I really would like to have one of those.

SHANE: Have? Have? You want to buy one? Hell, man, you have to *be* your own orgasm.

THE STUDENT: [*Timidly*] How?

SHANE: First you contract into your outer self, then you extend into your inner self.

THE STUDENT: [*Timidly*] How?

SHANE: By means of a group mind merger. Phase one: the anti-event. In a bourgeois event, this happens . . .

BRIGHT *brings May's baby from the cradle to* SHANE. SHANE *tosses the baby to* MAY, *who catches it. He coaxes it back out of her arms.*

MARKO: A completely totalitarian sequence.

Now SHANE *mimes tossing the baby to* MAY, *but without letting go of it. She clutches at space, misses, screams and falls to her knees sobbing.* SHANE *tosses the baby high to* DOOLEY.

DOOLEY: To be or not to be is to be is not to be . . . [*He deposits the baby in the lavatory.*] Is not to be is to be . . .

SHANE: Silence! No script, no roles, no dramatists, no directors, no professionalism.

SALLY: [*Rising and pursuing* DOOLEY] Give me a happening . . . [*She corners him on the wallbars and climbs all over him.*]

DOOLEY: Fact fantasy fact fantasy fact fantasy . . .

SHANE: Too many words. Words are corpses. [*Seizing and twisting* MARKO'S *arm.*] I abhor the fascism of a neatly finished phrase.

SALLY: [*Screaming*] He's going soft on me, he's going soft. He's a soft dildo. [DOOLEY *slumps to the ground.* SALLY *catches hold of a* STUDENT *and presses herself against him.*]

SHANE: [*To the student*] Take her, man. The bourgeois wishes to own what he sees but he cannot see what he does not own. Take her.

The STUDENT *slumps to the floor on top of* SALLY. *And now, as if wandering into a dream, into a waxworks, enter* MAX, FRANK, TOM, ANN, GARFIELD. *Other* STUDENTS *stand in the doorway.*

SHANE: [*Approaching the invaders*] Welcome, come on in, join us, share the nirvana of the anti-theatre with us . . .

Confrontation

TOM: Quite a performance.

MAX: [*To* BRIGHT] Theatre of total collapse, eh?

FRANK: Filth.

GARFIELD: [*To* BRIGHT] How much do they pay you to do this?

BRIGHT: The C.I.A., you mean?

GARFIELD: You said it.

BRIGHT: No doubt my complete exposure was only a matter of time.

GARFIELD: When we moved out of this theatre, the equipment was not smashed nor were guards put on the doors. Your students trusted you. So you immediately abuse their trust by setting it up as a garbage can for hippies, drop-outs, addicts and every available form of human refuse.

BRIGHT: Is it your intention that under the new Reign of Virtue all cultural activity should cease and the theatre fall into disuse?

GARFIELD: Did no rumour reach you that we are under siege?

BRIGHT: I am too old for gladiatorial spectacles.

FRANK: But not too old to discredit our movement.

ANN: [*Indicating* SALLY *and* MARKO] What's this doing here . . . and this? [*To* MAY] May, you should be ashamed.

BRIGHT: I understood that the Free University had opened its gates.

ANN: Not to whores and their pimps.

BRIGHT: I merely observed with interest a certain philosophical tendency among a minority of students.
GARFIELD: Which you actively promoted and encouraged.
BRIGHT: Since the majority of my regular drama students have deserted this theatre for higher things, I could see no harm in giving my time to those who wished to make use of it.
FRANK: They're a swarm of doped-up nuts and you know it. You hoped to attract the attention of the press. I can see the headlines and photographs: 'Student Power Means Student Orgy'.
GARFIELD: You have thrown in your lot with the counter-revolution.

BRIGHT *approaches* DOOLEY, *still on his lavatory.*

BRIGHT: [*Youthfully*] Tell me, comrade, why do we not permit exhibitions of formalistic and abstract art in the People's Republic?
DOOLEY: [*Sitting up straight, speaking as commissar*] Because the toiling masses have unanimously rejected such decadent productions, and because the toiling masses, if exposed to their influence, would be seriously corrupted.
BRIGHT: Thank you, comrade.

Pause.

GARFIELD: The so-called Anti-University is liquidated.
SHANE: Why don't you guys push off and wallow in your own hang-ups. Go rule the world. Leave us alone.
DOOLEY: If your bowels won't open, seize power.

TOM *knocks* DOOLEY *off his lavatory.*

MAX: [*To* BRIGHT] Get this rabble out of here. [*To* DOOLEY] And take your crap bin with you.

Resentful and lethargic, the Anti-University contingent depart, except for SHANE, *who displays his contempt by stretching out on the floor. No one cares to try and move him.*

GARFIELD: This theatre is closed indefinitely. Understood?

ANN: We trusted you, Steven.

BRIGHT: You occupied my theatre. Yes, *my* theatre. The theatre which, but for me, would never have risen from the soil.

TOM: In the heat of the struggle –

BRIGHT: Anything can be justified. That's one reason why I'm against heat. In any case, you are all taking this too seriously . . . a harmless diversion . . . a private charade . . . a mere pantomime – [GARFIELD *has meanwhile opened* BRIGHT'S *cupboards and begun to remove his notes and manuscripts. The* STUDENTS *assist willingly.*] What do you think you're doing?

GARFIELD: Do you know what the students in Japan do to ageing academic renegades and revisionists? Count yourself fortunate, Bright, that you are not in Japan. But no more charades, and no more pantomimes.

BRIGHT: [*Pushing towards* GARFIELD *but physically restrained by the* STUDENTS.] Leave those papers alone, you bastard! They're mine!

GARFIELD: For the time being they belong to the collective.

BRIGHT: But they're bound to get lost or damaged. [*To the* STUDENTS] You don't understand what you're doing. That's a life's work!

GARFIELD: Pity the man whose life can be held under my arm.

BRIGHT: [*Desperate now*] Max, Ann, please, I implore you . . . forget . . . I mean remember . . . I have done nothing to justify this barbarism. I'm not against you . . . Ann . . . Max . . . I was never among your enemies, I'm full of enthusiasm for your revolution, I mean . . . I only ask . . . all I ask . . . I ask only that you leave me in peace.

MAX: No man is an island.

BRIGHT: [*Turning away*] Ha! So much for your proud claim that your revolution is different. So much for your talk about transcending alienation; so much for your chatter about freedom living in the nerves and cells of your movement. It's not enough, you know, to be in the right camp.

GARFIELD: [*Departing, followed by the* STUDENTS] It's up to you, Bright.

MAX: [*Imitating* BRIGHT *as drama professor*] What an appalling line. A melodramatic extravaganza. [*The* STUDENTS *laugh.*]

BRIGHT *makes one further futile effort to get at his manuscripts, then stumbles into his own space.*

BRIGHT: The text, the text, if only I could see the text. Which scene are we in, which page are we on? [*He gropes, trying to recall the location of a line he has just delivered.*] 'it's not enough, you know, to be in the right camp.' Act two, Scene two? Yes! The students steal Bright's manuscripts . . . Then what? [*He gropes again.*] Ah! [*He speaks now as if mad.*] Take your realities for dreams! Yes!

SCENE THREE

The University theatre has been reoccupied. Bandaged heads, arms in slings and other signs of street warfare are in evidence. The general mood is fatigued and subdued.

MAX: As far as we can calculate . . . [*Noise continues*]

FRANK: [*Banging a table*] Quiet, damn it! [*The noise subsides*]

MAX: As far as we can calculate –

SHANE: Wait a moment. The Committee has not been re-elected for three days. Seems to me some comrades on the Committee are beginning to cultivate their own personalities.

GARFIELD: I would remind comrades that we are in the front line and under fire.

SHANE: Oh sure! First principle: the front-line is no place for elections. Second principle: a revolutionary is always in the front line.

General argument.

MAX: [*Wearily*] Shall I continue? Believe me, I'd rather go to bed.

VOICES: Continue.

A VOICE: [*Ironically*] Speak for England!

MAX: As far as we can calculate, thirty-two of us were arrested during yesterday's demonstration.

A STUDENT: We must demonstrate against that as well.

TOM: Three senior members of the Law Faculty have done a great job defending our people. I think we owe them a message of thanks.

MAX: The other thing concerns medical help. Ten of our first-aid team were beaten up by the police yesterday. So we need more volunteers. Don't volunteer if you believe in the Geneva Convention. [*Some hands are raised*]

FRANK: You all probably know what happened in California yesterday. Ninety arrests, three deaths. All of them blacks, naturally. A demonstration of protest will take place outside the American Embassy tomorrow afternoon.

Silence.

TOM: We must go. International solidarity is essential.

A STUDENT: There have been hundreds of demonstrations against the war and against police repression. The war goes on, and so does the police repression.

TOM: Then we must go on too.

A VOICE: Why?

TOM: Because government is a full-time occupation. Making money is a full-time occupation. Exploitation, mass murder and imperialism are full-time occupations. But protest only happens once a month, on Sundays. It's something the citizen fits in, when he can. Governments rely on that.

Silence.

ANN: I think many of us are rather tired. Some of us have hardly slept all week.

GARFIELD: Tom is right – in principle. But we have to be practical. We are already stretched to the limit. The defence of the University is our main responsibility.

A STUDENT: The war is more important than the University.

GARFIELD: The University is here and the war is ten thousand miles away.

FRANK: The war is everywhere. The war lives inside people.

GARFIELD: In that case, we challenge the system and the values behind the war by fighting here.

VOICES: I agree. That makes sense.

TOM: Some people seem to imagine that we could really defend the University against tanks. If we merely guard our own nest, we may as well call it a day.

VOICES: Hear, hear! He's right! No sell-out!

MAX: Let's get the sense of the meeting. Those against joining the demonstration at the embassy? [*Many hands go up*] Those in favour? [*A similar proportion of hands are raised*] I refuse to count. We don't believe in majorities of one. [*Sadly*] The general will, comrades, is in eclipse.

Silence.

ANN: Can I say something? I'm afraid I'm not going to be popular, I mean, we seem to be cutting ourselves off from reality. We were the first university to go over to the revolution. Five others followed. All five have now collapsed. We've done quite well. We occupied the buildings. We threw out the administration. No exams have been held. But what now? Can we sit here all summer? What do we hope to achieve?

Silence.

A GIRL STUDENT: I think Ann is right.

A STUDENT: [*Angrily*] There it is, the voice of sell-out. What did we hope to achieve when we started?

Rising tide of voices.

TOM: What do you propose, Ann? Do we crawl on hands and knees to the President? Do we say to him: promise us a commission of inquiry, promise us participation, promise us you'll see the light?

A STUDENT: Some people won't be satisfied until we're all in jail, hospital or the morgue.

A VOICE: Nihilism is nonsense.

GARFIELD: No compromise, no sell-out!

ANN: [*Raising her voice*] Negotiation needn't involve capitulation.

MAX: I agree with Ann. All along we have refused to negotiate. They have wanted to talk to us, but we have said no. That's fine while the revolution is in the ascendant. But if the movement is now contracting and the working class has failed to respond to our initiative –

A VOICE: No, no, take your dreams for realities!

MAX: [*Shouting*] I detest empty rhetoric!

General uproar. MAX, FRANK, TOM *and* GARFIELD *confer.*

TOM: [*Holding up his hand*] We need time to cool off. I suggest we break up now into groups and cells which can discuss the situation more rationally. We'll meet again in general assembly at six this evening.

The meeting breaks up rapidly. MAX, FRANK, TOM, ANN *and* GARFIELD *are left alone. Despondent silence.*

GARFIELD: [*Irritably*] Ann, you ought to resign from the Committee.

MAX: Why should she?

GARFIELD: Because she's not in sympathy with our general policy.

MAX: Policy is a creation not an inheritance.

ANN: I'm quite prepared to go along with the majority. I'm not opting out.

GARFIELD: The Committee exists to lead, not to follow.

MAX: Well! So now we know!

GARFIELD: Don't speak to me like that.

MAX: Sorry, professor.

TOM: Hey! Cool it, please.

FRANK: Ann is entitled to say what she thinks.

Tense silence. Enter BRIGHT *cautiously.*

GARFIELD: No one invited you here. What do you want?

BRIGHT: My life's work.

GARFIELD: You're out of luck.

MAX: He's hoping to capitalise on our difficulties.

GARFIELD: We have no difficulties.

MAX: What did you have in mind?

BRIGHT: Ah. Well, since you ask, the Annual Theatre Congress opens in ten days' time. [*He faces about*] In some respects it's not unlike the Frankfurt Book Fair – with young actors up for auction instead of books. [*Pause*]

MAX: So?

BRIGHT: It's all a little sad. The talent scouts and the critics, you appreciate, well, much as they respect my judgement, like to see the display for themselves. [*Pause*]

TOM: But this year there will be no display.

BRIGHT: [*Shrugging*] So I shall have to tell them.

MAX: Which means that we must rely on testimonials from our distinguished teacher.

BRIGHT: Your what? Do such animals exist in your brave new world?

ANN: Steven, we are still your students.

BRIGHT: Ha! Ha! [*Pause*] Where are my notes and manuscripts? You have propelled me into the seventh age of man when I should be only in the fifth. [*Pause*] As things now stand, I can offer no opinions on your individual qualities as actors. I cannot even grade you. You will leave the University without any final degree.

Long silence.

MAX: I don't see how we can put together a production now.

FRANK: Our final production has been running all week. That is all we have to offer.

TOM: To reduce it now to stage proportions would be simply to embalm ourselves.

BRIGHT: Agreed. I had a different play in mind. [*Pause*]

GARFIELD: The theatre is closed, and that's final.

BRIGHT: The Gods didn't close it.

MAX: [*To* BRIGHT] *Pentagon 67*?

GARFIELD: *Pentagon 67*! Another cunning diversion.

BRIGHT: The Pentagon is the opposite of a diversion. All political roads lead to the Pentagon. Throughout the world demonstrators protest outside embassies, airfields and recruiting centres. All substitutes for Satan's castle – for the Pentagon.

GARFIELD: For you, the Pentagon is a five-sided piece of cardboard suspended by wires from pulleys. Exit life, enter art.

BRIGHT: Art, at its best, is revelation, perception, demonstration. That, after all, is what you have practised here. You don't have rockets and anti-tank guns in your armoury. What you have – potentially at least – is an authentic sense of theatre. All I suggest is that you continue the same struggle – in a slightly modified medium.

GARFIELD: All he wants is to see a bunch of cynical dealers look you over like horse flesh and wave cheque books under your noses.

TOM: *Pentagon 67* has a large cast. It involves practically the whole of the Drama School. If we start rehearsals now, the University will be left virtually undefended. The police can just walk in and arrest the lot of us.

GARFIELD: That is no doubt the intention.

Pause.

BRIGHT: I have spoken to the President.

GARFIELD: He admits it!

BRIGHT: They are all desperate for a face-saving formula: our President, the Secretary of State for Education, the Prime Minister. I offered them a formula; the President clutched at it. A resumption of rehearsals will be accepted as a return to normality. The police will vanish from the gates.

GARFIELD: And there will be no arrests, no expulsions, no sackings?

BRIGHT: None at all.

GARFIELD: They gave you their word. They are all honourable men.

FRANK: Look what happened in France: total repression.

BRIGHT: France is France, England is England.

Long silence.

GARFIELD: Can't you see the satisfaction he's getting out of all this? After all those years of being idolised by his students, suddenly young people developed their own values, suddenly action replaced words, suddenly he was swept aside. He became obsolete.

BRIGHT: All true. I have an interest in preserving the University from chaos; both the chaos of anarchy and the chaos of outside repression. If you imagine that the President wishes me well, you are mistaken. If there is a purge here, Bright's head will be the first to fall into the basket.

MAX: [*Sulkily*] What reforms do they offer?

BRIGHT: Good God Max, would you be satisfied with vague promises? In any case, do you *want* reforms?

Silence.

ANN: I think Steven's proposal makes sense.

MAX: I don't know.

GARFIELD: You don't know. Have you forgotten what the President and his minions are like? Have you forgotten what brought you to this? [*To* MAX, FRANK, TOM, *and* ANN]. You suspended, you suspended, you suspended, you expelled. Have you forgotten how the system works? It's just a cheap hoax.

BRIGHT: You have my notes and manuscripts. What better guarantee can I offer? [*He sees that the* STUDENTS *are almost won over*] By the way, I almost forgot. Mangin and Baumann are in town. As you know, they are co-organisers of the International Festival of Student Drama which is to take place next month in Paris and West Berlin. They are both ecstatic about your revolution. [*Pause*] They have room for one additional production from this country. [*The* STUDENTS *listen intently*]

GARFIELD: [*Enraged*] Ping! A half crown in the box. Wait for the five pound note. [*Exit in despair*]

BRIGHT: What can I say? Your production of *Pentagon 67* in Paris and Berlin would no doubt generate what Mangin calls *un scandal explosif* and Baumann calls *einen Ausbruch.* How can I explain to them that you have better things to do? If, as they insist, this would be the first time that revolutionary inspiration had come from England to the Continent, how can I get across to them that you are more interested in staging punch-ups round the main gate? [*Confident, he goes to the door*] After all, a man can only explain what he can comprehend.

He exits

SCENE FOUR

A curtain has been lowered, front-stage, in such a manner as to emphasise the fact that we are about to see a theatrical performance, Pentagon 67. *The curtain might be painted in the style of a sixteenth-century map of the world or mariner's chart. It represents the Pentagon as the centre of the universe. U.S. men of war and machines of war cavort towards Vietnam in the pictorial style of the old ships, sailors, whales and lighthouses. Dotted about in piratical postures are hippies and protesters. Cherubs, sporting helicopter wings, guard the passage of the glory boys through hailstorms of red stars. And so on.*

The curtain rises. On the screen, centre, as in Act One, Scene One a projection of the Pentagon. A line of SOLDIERS *is drawn up, rear left, behind a white rope some three feet from the ground. The helmeted* SOLDIERS *carry slung rifles and night sticks in their hands. From their belts hang chains and black tear gas containers.*

What we shall see is an uninterrupted dress rehearsal of Pentagon 67. *The directorial hand of* BRIGHT *must be abundantly evident. The more potentially naturalistic an episode, the more notably stylised and alienated should be its actual execution. We must feel in* BRIGHT'S *method that persistant 'holding back' to which his militant drama students have become allergic. And we should also feel – subtly, never overtly – their rejection as student actors of the roles they are now playing.*

Apart from the line of SOLDIERS, *the stage is empty. Enter two* BLACK MILITANTS. *They saunter up to the* NEGRO *among the* SOLDIERS.

1ST BLACK MILITANT: Hey Nigger . . .
2ND BLACK MILITANT: Hey shoe shine boy . . .
1ST BLACK MILITANT: Nigger – no Vietnamese ever called me nigger – nigger.
2ND BLACK MILITANT: How's nigger heaven, nigger soldier?
1ST BLACK MILITANT: Hey nigger, when did you last kiss Mr Charlie's white one?
2ND BLACK MILITANT: Going to be a nigger hero in Mr Charlie's Vietnam war?
1ST BLACK MILITANT: You're really some man, Mr Pig . . .
2ND BLACK MILITANT: Hey nigger pig, give us some pigskin . . .

The NEGRO SOLDIER *hangs his head and is quickly pulled out of the line by the* SERGEANT *of the guard.* [*The* BLACK MILITANTS *in this episode can be played equally well by black actors or by white ones with blackened faces.*]

SERGEANT: [*To* BLACK MILITANTS] You guys want your head busted right now and I'll do it.

The BLACK MILITANTS *give ground. Enter now two columns which converge: the* YOUNG MILITANTS, *carrying SDS, Resistance Movement, Peace and Freedom banners, etc., and a contingent of* HIPPIES].

VOICE OF MONITOR: [*On megaphone*] Will you please sit down. Please be seated. We have made a pledge to the authorities to remain seated.

But before the young people have fully complied, through the crowd bursts the well-known novelist JAMES PACK, *accompanied by a* REPORTER *whose microphone is always within inches of* PACK'S *mouth.* PACK *is spry, energetic, and wearing a smart three piece suit.*

CROWD VOICES: It's Jim Pack,
Publicity hound,

The Great American Novelist,
Pulitzer Prize 1984.

PACK: [*Addressing the crowd*] Fellow Americans! The war we are conducting in Vietnam is the arsehole of our collective psyche. It's obscene . . .

VOICE: You should know . . .

PACK: I do know. I know because I write obscene books. I tell you this war is more obscene than all the dirty books that all the dirty writers like myself could ever write. [*Pause*] Incidentally, I'm as full of crap as LBJ is, it's just that I prefer my own.

JOURNALIST: Why are you here, Mr Pack?

PACK: I am here to protest the obscene war by committing an intensely symbolic act of – protest. Come what may, I intend to get the other side of that rope.

VOICE: [*Derisively*] We're waiting, Jim.

PACK: Hold it. Where's my goddam obscene lawyer? [*Shouting*] Marty, where are ya?

MARTY, *a Jewish lawyer, hurries up, panting.*

MARTY: Jim, we're out of luck. The US Attorney was less than friendly. I said to him: Sir, Mr Pack will accept a thirty dollar fine and a warning. He will also plead *Nolo Contendere*. He said to me: Boy, I was born and raised in Alabama. Tell your client that the dirtiest four-letter word we know in Alabama is Pack.

PACK: So no deal, huh?

MARTY: None, Jim . . .

PACK: [*To crowd*] The last existentialist hero of American literature gives way to no man. [*Grabs* MARTY]. Now get this straight, Marty, either I come out of Occoquan jail in time to catch the six o'clock shuttle back to New York, or you're fired. Dolores is giving a party for five hundred in Washington Square and I mean to be there. [*Facing the rope*] Okay, let's not hang about. No, wait. One of those kids over there is holding a Vietcong flag. It's Middle

America we have to reach. [*Calls across the crowd*] Hey, Ho Chi Minh . . . look to your flies, son.

1ST YOUNG MILITANT: Say, Jim, I mean when you write up this story tomorrow, how much do you think it will catch? One hundred thousand or two hundred thousand?

PACK: A million. I'm not afraid of money.

2ND YOUNG MILITANT: Tell Middle America how the young let you down, how the blacks got under your skin and how the workers turned fascist just to disappoint you.

1ST YOUNG MILITANT: Tell them of the agonies of being a middle-aged disenchanted leftist conservative.

HIPPIE: Hurry, Jim, or you'll miss the scuttle flight back to New York.

PACK: If any of ya want to fight, just step this way. I never throw the first punch. [*He turns and attempts to climb over the white rope, but he finds it uncomfortably high. Then he tries to crawl underneath it, but finds it uncomfortably low. Finally he is helped over it by derisive* MILITANTS. *The* SOLDIERS *grab him.*] Okay fellas, take it easy, I'm not resisting arrest.

JOURNALIST: Mr Pack, will you please tell the American people why you have done this?

PACK: I have attempted to penetrate the arsehole of the Pentagon to protest Uncle Sam's whorehouse war.

PACK *is arrested and led away, followed by* JOURNALISTS, *etc. Long silence. Gently pushing other demonstrators aside, the* HIPPIES *form a circle centre stage.*

1ST HIPPIE: Friends, now is the time.

2ND HIPPIE: A license was requested of the authorities. Many hundreds of gallant diggers and other gentle spirits offered to encircle the Pentagon. In the name of revolutionary alchemy.

HIPPIES: [*Chanting gently*] The Pentagon, the Pentagon.

3RD HIPPIE: License refused.

1ST HIPPIE: But we shall overcome.

HIPPIES: We shall overcome.

They now produce their own Pentagon. How this is to be done each company of actors may decide. In the Nottingham production five HIPPIES *lay stretched out on the floor, forming a pentagon, with five others kneeling in prayer at the five corners. When the moment of levitation arrived, the prostrate* HIPPIES *writhed without succeeding in raising themselves from the ground. Music accompanies the ceremony, oriental and on a monotone throughout: an Indian triangle, a cymbal, finger bells.*

1ST HIPPIE: We call upon all the powers of the cosmos to join our souls . . .
HIPPIES: We call upon all the powers of the cosmos . . .
1ST HIPPIE: To shelter our rite . . .
HIPPIES: To shelter our rite . . .
1ST HIPPIE: In the name of Jehovah, Osiris, Shiva-Shakra, Dionysus, Isis and Buddha . . .
HIPPIES: And in the name . . .
1ST HIPPIE: Of the soldiers killed in Vietnam . . .
2ND HIPPIE: Our soldiers.
HIPPIES: Our soldiers.
1ST HIPPIE: Their soldiers.
HIPPIES: Their soldiers.
3RD HIPPIE: Who are also our soldiers.
1ST HIPPIE: In the name of what cannot be named . . .
HIPPIES: The unnamable.
1ST HIPPIE: We call upon and invoke the one true spirit . . .
HIPPIES: It is you, it is you . . .
1ST HIPPIE: We call upon the spirit to levitate the Pentagon from its curse of damnation.
HIPPIES: It is you, it is you . . .
1ST HIPPIE: Out devils out, out devils out . . .
HIPPIES: Out, out, out . . .
2ND HIPPIE: Out generals out, out murderers out . . .
HIPPIES: Out, out, out . . .

The HIPPIES *drop their voices to a whisper.*

HIPPIES: Exorcise, levitate, exorcise, levitate . . .

The prostrate HIPPIES *writhe and then subside.*

2ND HIPPIE: [*Approaching* SOLDIERS] All evil spirits have fled. Soldiers, brothers in love, your bad war, your bad dream . . . has ended. Lay down your arms.

The SERGEANT *of the guard swiftly clubs him to the ground. Cry of horror from the crowd. The* HIPPIES *wail pathetically and carry their man away.*

1ST HIPPIE: Okay then, ten thousand children will instigate loot-ins at department stores. Our children will expose the property fetish that sustains genocidal war.

HIPPIE GIRLS *approach the soldiers and bare their breasts in a way which is both brazen and innocent.*

HIPPIES: [*Pathetically*] Join us, soldiers, share our love, share our joys, share our girls . . .

Silence as the GIRLS *press against the* SOLDIERS.

A SOLDIER: Share our girls! Why, they're all faggots!

SERGEANT: Silence, trooper, hold your tongue. [*to the* GIRLS.] Step back there. [*The* GIRLS *merely expose themselves further.*] I warn ya, step back, ya indecent whores. [*The* SERGEANT *hesitates, succumbs to emotion, and clubs a* GIRL *to the ground. The crowd react violently. The* SERGEANT *bellows to his men.*] B Company, hold your ground, hold that line.

MILITANTS: [*Mocking him*] Hold that line, hold that line.

A MILITANT (MAX): Okay, so now you've all seen what the system is really like. That [*Pointing to the* SERGEANT] is the system.

A MILITANT (FRANK): We've got to organise and we've got to fight.

A MILITANT (TOM): They use force, we must do the same.
A GIRL (ANN): No, no. Don't surrender to their subhuman logic. We don't want to become like them. Don't you see – that's what they hope will happen.
A MILITANT (MAX): [*Trying to rouse the crowd*] We didn't come here to levitate the Pentagon, nor to weep in silent vigil outside the Pentagon. We came here to seize and destroy the Pentagon.
MILITANTS: [*Urging on the crowd*] That's right . . .
We have the numbers,
We have the justice,
Who's a chicken, who's a chicken,
Only chickens sit, only chickens sit . . .

A section of the crowd begins to surge forward. But among others uncertainty, confusion and fear prevail.

SERGEANT: [*On Bullhorn*]: Back, back, back! Hold that line at all costs, soldiers, hold that line.

The helicopter swoops low overhead and hovers. The MILITANTS *temporarily lose their cohesion.*

1ST GIRL (ANN): We need leadership, that's what we need.
2ND GIRL: Isn't there somebody here who can talk to us, someone we all respect?
A MILITANT: Respectable America is some place else.
A YOUNG MAN: [*softly*] We have no leader. Che is dead.
A MILITANT: [*With book*] I'd like to read you what Lenin said . . .
VOICES: Lenin is dead too. Let him rest in peace.
1ST GIRL (ANN): In my opinion there is only one philosopher in America today who makes any kind of sense. And that's Karl Steinblitz.
A MILITANT (MAX): Steinblitz ought to be with us today. If he really believes what he teaches, he ought to be here.

An elderly, scholarly gentleman comes into view. His demeanour is both proud and faintly saint-like. This is KARL STEINBLITZ. *But the role of* STEINBLITZ *in* Pentagon 67 *is obviously played by* BRIGHT. *As* STEINBLITZ *is recognised an awed silence descends over all parts of the crowd.*

STEINBLITZ: My name is Karl Steinblitz.

Awed hush.

VOICES: Give us the word
Should we attempt to storm the Pentagon here and now?
Speak, speak . . .

STEINBLITZ: [*With a gesture commanding silence*] I am an old man now, an old professor. Old professors like to lay down the law and no one interrupts. Nowadays in America such arrogance is no longer permitted. [*Pause*] Of course it is to your generation that we must now turn. You are the vanguard of the new society.

VOICE: Give us a lead, sir.

STEINBLITZ: A lead? There are so many misunderstandings. I blame myself. I write something on paper, it is printed and distributed, and very soon it comes back to me in a most peculiar shape – a kind of totem pole of slogans and magic symbols. This invariably means that the New Left has adopted my position. So I ask myself: do not these young radicals perhaps reflect the prevailing totalitarian mindlessness; is not their culture also based on love of what is physical, transitory, instantaneous? Does not a problem arise when the revolutionary vanguard feeds off simplifications alone?

A VOICE: What should we do here and now?

STEINBLITZ: 'What should we do now?' Always this now. Pop. Pop art, pop thought, pop theatre, pop revolution. Pop. Even your conception of what you call the 'system' is a form of pop sociology. Pop. How often your demonstrations remind me of certain primitive rituals of cleansing and catharsis . . .

Outbursts of indignation among the young MILITANTS.

MILITANTS: You are old, old.
The action of philosophy must be the philosophy of action.
The philosophers have only interpreted the world.
We mean to change it.
We all know what Che would have done.

STEINBLITZ: I hear the words 'Che Guevara' pass frequently from your mouths. I hear some of you transferring his theories from the third world to the first, from the jungles to the cities. You call yourselves urban guerrillas. But perhaps you overlook one important attribute of this Argentinian – his pragmatism, his sense of direction, his feeling for detail. Guevara was a technician of revolution: do you deserve the title? No, you lust after the romantic apocalypse. [*Outburst of anger in the crowd.*] There are no hippies in the third world.

Uproar.

VOICES: What do you really know about life?
When did you last feel something, touch something, fuck something?
We do not honour you.
Back to your books,
Back Back Back Back!

STEINBLITZ *suddenly smiles and nods, as if in agreement. As if, perhaps, he had all along been baiting them as a prelude to joining them. The crowd falls silent again, expecting a lead.*

STEINBLITZ: As you see, I am a very rude old man. And I notice that I am not in favour with the angels. Even so, I offer you one final reflection. In the ancient classical tragedy, the hero, the great protagonist, the fount and focus of power, dominated the stage. He was there, accessible to our eyes and ears, fully revealing his motives and manoeuvres. Such a form of theatre, with its great love of mimesis and illusion, reflected a political reality. Power, real power, lay in a few hands. But this reality is no more, my friends, it is dead, gone . . . yet you behave as if it were. You speak of LBJ as if he were Richard III. But is not the real tragedy of our age, the real alienation, that of emptiness and absence? Our demon always lies out of reach; only his shadows are visible, like the shadows of clouds racing across the sun. And so you fight these shadows – the soldiers who confront you now, the police of the cities, the President. You ask: should we storm the Pentagon? Ah! The Pentagon, today's demon, today's shadow. Suppose for a moment it were physically possible, which I doubt. Suppose indeed that you seized the generals and dismantled their war machines; suppose you invaded the White House and did what you dream of doing to its principal occupant. What then? Does not the empty space remain? It does. But that space was made by man and what man makes he can unmake, if only he knows where to search. Where? Did you ever see the pall of smoke hanging day and night over Detroit, Manchester or Karlsruhe? Did you ever watch a Wall Street teleprinter spewing out is endless tape of avarice? Did you ever give serious consideration to what that smoke and that tape represent? Capitalism, you reply. 'The System', you say. If such answers satisfy you, you will never comprehend man's long undeclared war on himself. [*Pause*] I see that you do not relish what I have to say. I shall accept your advice, I shall go back to my books.

Silence prevails as STEINBLITZ *walks off slowly. The spell is finally broken by the voice of a* SOLDIER, *almost a whisper, yet loud in the silence.*

SOLDIER: Now that's a guy you can respect. He's got education.

The spell is broken. A young MILLITANT (MAX) *leaps forward.*

MILITANT (MAX): Burn a draft card and keep warm!

He burns his draft card. Cheers from the crowd. Others do the same. Growing excitement. The SERGEANT *of the guard issues warnings, the helicopter descends again. The light is fading. Now the* MILITANTS *join arms and surge forward through and past the* SOLDIERS. *The stage empties. As in Act One, Scene One, a projection on the screen of an interior corridor of the Pentagon. A* YOUNG MAN *and a* YOUNG WOMAN (MAX *and* ANN) *appear breathless.*

YOUNG MAN: We've made it. We're inside.

YOUNG WOMAN: There were no guards. Where were the guards?

YOUNG MAN: Gone home, I guess. Or maybe . . .

YOUNG WOMAN: On the outside it has five corners, but inside it has no shape at all, just corridors and more corridors.

YOUNG MAN: Each room is like the next, nothing but telephones and piles of paper.

YOUNG WOMAN: But no people. No people anywhere. The place is empty.

YOUNG MAN: There's nothing to lay your hands on, nothing to seize, no one to grab hold of. Nothing to do.

YOUNG WOMAN: Then how does it work . . . how does it run the war if . . .

YOUNG MAN: Look out!

Two shadowy figures emerge from the surrounding darkness and seize the YOUNG MAN *and* YOUNG WOMAN. *Then sounds of general fighting, shouts backstage. The lights go up suddenly. What we find is* MAX *and* ANN, *as well as*

FRANK *and* TOM, *held and handcuffed not by Pentagon guards but by London* POLICE CONSTABLES. *Enter a* POLICE SUPERINTENDENT *with the* PRESIDENT *of the University. The helicopter is heard hovering low . . . not over the Pentagon but over the University. Finally* BRIGHT *enters, divesting himself of the appearance and personality of* STEINBLITZ.

TOM: Bastard.

MAX: [*To* BRIGHT] You must be very sick.

FRANK: So much for revolutionary inspiration travelling from this country to the Continent.

ANN: We always intended to return your wretched manuscripts. They are quite safe.

BRIGHT: You remind me of Arab shepherds clutching at Dead Sea Scrolls – meaningless to them, but worth a price. [*Pause*] After all I had done for you.

TOM: Betraying us is hardly the best way of getting them back.

BRIGHT: [*Apparently not worried about his papers*] I wanted to prove how quickly you would betray yourselves. Only one thing motivated you – you who protest so loudly that the University has become a factory for manufacturing elites, a springboard for comfortable careers. What wouldn't you do in the name of your revolution? Steal a man's life's work. Close down his theatre. Burn down London? Very probably. But would you sacrifice your own futures, those rosy dreams of playing Coriolanus, Hamlet or Rosalind at the Old Vic? No. The doctors, technicians, civil servants and managers – their ambitions are despicable. But not yours. [*Pause*] Here endeth the glorious revolution. [*He walks away and fiddles with the stage lighting*]

SUPERINTENDENT: [*To* PRESIDENT] Shall I take these people in, now?

BRIGHT: [*Changing mood*] Don't play it up. [*To* SUPERINTENDENT] Enough is enough. [*To* STUDENTS] My modest happening is now closed. After all, you always insist that action speaks louder than words. I don't see why we shouldn't go to the Drama Festival – provided you can contain yourselves. The talent scouts will be here tomorrow evening. Meanwhile, I have recommended most of you as gilt-edged investments for the professional theatre. Anyone with a modicum of talent who studies under me is likely to go a long way. [*He smiles. To everyone*] Okay, stow your costumes and don't hang about. [*Pause*] By the way, where are my manuscripts? [*They all stare at him in amazement. He speaks to the* CONSTABLES] Take off these ludicrous medieval shackles. [*No one moves. He speaks to the* PRESIDENT] What's the problem? Do you feel you haven't justified your part unless you make a speech?

SUPERINTENDENT: [*To* PRESIDENT] What's his line, sir?

PRESIDENT: I don't know. He's – eccentric.

BRIGHT: An actor who can't stop acting is an insult to the theatre. [*He examines the* SUPERINTENDENT *more closely*] Who are you, anyway? [*He tries to pull off the* SUPERINTENDENT'S *moustache*].

SUPERINTENDENT: Professor, I must warn you. [*He takes an identity card from his inside pocket*]

BRIGHT: [*Taking the card*] Well, if this isn't decadence. He carries a card *inside* his coat. I have no patience with method acting.

BRIGHT *becomes agitated. He rushes at the* PRESIDENT *and attempts to rub the makeup off his face. None comes. The* PRESIDENT *turns away in disgust. The* SUPERINTENDENT *extends his arm and flicks his fingers, demanding the return of his card.* BRIGHT *yields it. His collapse is now complete.*

SUPERINTENDENT: [*To* CONSTABLES] Come on, then.

BRIGHT: But this is England. This is London. [*Pause.*] This is a university.

FRANK: Your England.

TOM: Your London.
MAX: Your university.

The CONSTABLES *are pulling the* STUDENTS *away.*

BRIGHT: [*Hurrying after* MAX] My manuscripts! Where are they?

MAX: Tell the Property Department to make you some more.

BRIGHT *is left alone with the* PRESIDENT. BRIGHT *is stricken and immobile. The* PRESIDENT *advances on him slowly. Helicopter.*

THE END